Light Within

Light Within

The Inner Path of Meditation

LAURENCE FREEMAN OSB

Foreword by
Sir Yehudi Menuhin

CROSSROAD · NEW YORK

1987

The Crossroad Publishing Company
370 Lexington Avenue, New York, N.Y. 10017

© 1986 Laurence Freeman OSB
Foreword © 1986 Yehudi Menuhin

Printed in the United States of America

Library of Congress Catalog Card Number: 86-073221
ISBN: 0-8245-0830-0

Scriptural quotations are taken from the New English Bible,
second edition © 1970 by permission of Oxford and
Cambridge University Presses.

Contents

Foreword

May I, as a Jew by birth and background, comment on this guide to meditation? Perhaps I can best describe it as a guide for the reader to *himself*.

Father Laurence refers in his Introduction to the Catholic nun who went to a nomadic tribe in Africa which had 'resolutely resisted all attempts by Church and state at integration or evangelization'. The French missionary went only to serve and in doing so did *not* represent Church or State, but hoped that in serving their physical needs the tribe would come to feel a radiating selfless love emanating from her faith which they eventually might wish to share.

In the same spirit I would like to think of this book as a guide for those of all religions and even for those not claiming any particular religious label but apprehending and recognizing the ultimate Unknowable in the unity, the continuity, the interdependence within all creation.

The reader will understand why I believe it is possible to serve, equally committedly and selflessly, without necessarily evoking even to oneself names or nouns, by simply obeying and fulfilling that inspired awareness, be it intuitive, emotional or intellectual, that unites us to everything that lives, breathes, pulsates.

Greenpeace, the Prisoners of Conscience Fund, Amnesty International, the Red Cross, the wave of selfless sympathy for the starving in Ethiopia or the victims in Mexico, or those in South Africa, and a thousand other good works from Alcoholics Anonymous to Friends of the Earth are not necessarily done in the name of Jesus, however ideal a living symbol of goodness and wisdom he assuredly is.

Until the French Revolution we within our European background (overwhelmingly Christian as it is), allowed nothing to
happen, good or bad, except within Christian concepts. It is
wrong, however, to blame the Church for behaviour typical of
mankind the world over, for sins that would have been and are
perpetrated in the name of almost every set of beliefs, true or
false, prejudiced or superstitious, governing every section of
mankind. I feel that to claim the realm of love, or peace, or
meditation, or the possibility of redemption, forgiveness or
reward through any exclusive avenue or creed is no longer
realistic.

Human beings, as they are constituted, seem to require a
middle man, a broker, between them and that greater mystery,
'the spirit within our hearts and the way that is the truth'. No
one fulfills that role better than Jesus, the Jew, the innocent
man of truth who died in Jerusalem at the hands of his own
people. (How many millions of innocent are being destroyed,
as I write these words, for and by the sins of all mankind?)
Certainly the crucified Jesus is, sadly, an apt symbol for the
senseless cruelties of our world.

Jesus, the living instrument of forgiveness – Buddha, a mirror
to the inscrutable wisdom of mystic union with the Infinite: yet
both approach each other, meet and overlap in their vows of
poverty, in their true wisdom, renunciation and compassion.
Father Laurence Freeman's message is decidedly not only to
Christians who are wedded to Christ, but to all those who are
committed to truth and beauty, who love one another and who
know the meaning of love spiritual and temporal. Sometimes
these loves relate or fuse into one. Sometimes the loves are
pagan or polygamous, sometimes monotheistic and monog-
amous, but they and we are always an expression of that dual
belonging to what we sense as temporal, and to what we sense
as eternal; in reality two concurrent journeys as might occur in
a particular boat which we long to share with a loved one on
an endless river.

Father Laurence is so right about simplicity, truth and meditation. In my own experience I know how misleading and

totally inept is the common phrase 'to break a bad habit'. This obsession with compulsion and with violence is a peculiarly 'human' characteristic. Very often terms such as 'strength of will', 'determination', 'violence', 'vengeance' are grossly misleading. Although courage is hardly a quality I would in any way wish to disparage, the surmounting of difficulties may often be as much through perseverance and patience in the ways of simplicity, poverty, clarity and quiet – through that zero point we used to call 'neutral' in non-automatic cars which we always had to pass in shifting between gears. We have come to believe that supreme effort and determination to achieve is the measure of our success and that nothing can happen without muscle power and force of will. The indomitable, the unflinching, the invincible: these are the hallmarks of our civilization. We believe in the exertion of the most and we have lost the understanding of the power in the subtlety of the least. It is only in going back repeatedly, every day, to a neutral point, to a meditative instant of balance, that we can explore that narrow space which exists between what may be called 'zero to one'. In returning to the silent and the empty we find the sources and the ways of strength. Strength is not the accumulation of tension and with it all the accompanying worry, anxiety and frustration piling up every day; strength is what comes if you build from zero. The most important part of the greatest strength is what happens between zero and one. Measure that space, measure it in its smallest diameter, acquire subtlety in the feeling of that enormous difference between zero and one and for the myriad degrees between zero and one.

When you do that then you will find one thousand, one million subtle gradations and you will always return to zero. Meditation is the exercise, or, if you wish, the lack of exercise, the 'minus' exercise which repeatedly makes you acquainted with that secret emptiness, the apparent vacuum which is then irresistibly filled with the abundance of your life, of existence, of the whole life, of the whole of the Universe, the power of the sun, of love, the importance of the atom.

I am thankful that Father Laurence Freeman recognizes the *no-role* of *not* trying, *not* doing, *not* fighting and rather *accepting* the blessed, patient, healing hands of grace, hope and joy within ourselves, as between ourselves; rejecting the poisons and toxins that come with those bad habits which put our whole being into imbalance, imposed through fear, ill health, frustration, impatience, dissatisfaction, disillusionment, greed and all that is sometimes called 'sin'.

To put the experience of meditation into old-fashioned words, it is truth 'to share a secret with God', without *understanding* the secret, yet enjoying a living communion with the greater Unknowable. It is to us in all humility a setting oneself apart in this deepest core of our being; apart from, independent of, unassailable by all the 'knowables' in daily life or the presumed knowables – for each has its mystery. This experience of meditation related to prayer, poetry and philosophy has been known to all the great religions.

Music, too, is a form of meditation. Instead of the mantra I may go through a score in my mind. It is unlike meditation because it is not an absence of thought or evocation, and yet it *does* remove one from the immediate world into the mind of a great composer. If that composer is a man of supreme vision then of course you share that experience with him. It is a learning process. It is a concentration and a release and an escape. It shares some of the qualities of meditation; and although it is not pure meditation it has given me moments of deep emotion, of ecstatic and almost mystical joy and moments profoundly moving, almost to tears. But again, to achieve this experience one is submitting humbly to the study and the emotion, the intellect of another mind, another heart, be it Beethoven's or Bartok's or Bach's; or for the poets, Shakespeare or Hölderlin; or for the scientists, Einstein or Darwin.

One's own life and one's own experience of happiness and tragedy serve to effect that deeper union with the composer's own emotions and intellect, for without our own experience we wouldn't quite understand what he is trying to say. Yet I found, because I played this music as a child, that even that experience at a tender age does not have to be spelt out in words and letters but simply comes. It exists probably already in the unborn child, that sense of infinity, of tragedy, of joy, of struggle and of dreams. These are the very elements of life which are then later spelt out, acted out, lived through; but they surely exist intrinsically in every living cell and surely in the child about to be born.

If I have dwelt rather long on my own thoughts about meditation, it is because I feel that this book is not meant to exclude those who have an intuitive and possibly unlabelled need, sense and hunger. Meditation need not be done only through Jesus or only in Buddha's name, or in any other name. It can just be. Be. Without a name.

London   YEHUDI MENUHIN
October 1985

How to Meditate

Sit down. Sit still and upright. Close your eyes lightly. Sit relaxed but alert. Silently, interiorly begin to say a single word. We recommend the prayer-phrase, 'Maranatha'. Recite it as four syllables of equal length. Listen to it as you say it, gently but continuously. Do not think or imagine anything – spiritual or otherwise. If thoughts and images come, these are distractions at the time of meditation, so keep returning to simply saying the word. Meditate each morning and evening for between twenty and thirty minutes.

Addresses of two meditation centres:

Christian Meditation Centre
29 Campden Hill Road
London W8 7DX
England
Tel: 01 937 0014

The Benedictine Priory
1475 Pine Avenue West
Montreal H3G 1B3
Canada
Tel: 514 849 2728

Introduction

I recently made the annual visit to the meditation groups in England which are part of the extended community of our small Montreal monastery. Just as we were about to begin Mass I was called away to the telephone. A French sister, a doctor with an Irish-based missionary congregation, was calling from the airport on her way back to Africa. She had wanted to be with the groups then meeting and asked to be remembered to them. In a few days she would be taking up her new assignment, following a nomadic tribe which had resolutely resisted all attempts by Church and state at integration or evangelization. She was going simply to be present to them in their physical needs firstly, but her presence would bring them into contact with the presence of Christ. Before she left to catch her plane she said how she was strengthened and sustained by being as faithful as she could to the way of the mantra. She asked us, using a favourite phrase of John Main who had introduced her to meditation, to 'keep me in your heart'.

The chapters in this book have been written from talks or conferences given to people living a far more ordinary vocation than that missionary sister's. Yet, like her, they are finding the way of meditation to be the way of access to the deepest spiritual strength necessary for their spiritual fidelity and continued growth as human beings. Because that spiritual strength and creative energy is the love of the glorified Jesus, a most wonderful and mysterious bond unites all those who encounter it, whether they fulfil the conditions of poverty and purity in the African bush or in a European or American suburb. In that bond of fellow-pilgrims, as co-disciples, we discover that there is one Christian vocation: to know, love and serve God in, with and through Jesus. As that discovery transforms our consciousness and gradually enlightens us, a curiously liberating paradox appears. We may seek the Spirit within our hearts because we know we will fail our human vocation without it; but encountering the Spirit realigns our priorities and resolves our contemplative–active dualities in such a way as to teach us that our vocation *is* to make this journey and this encounter. The Way *is* the Truth and this Truth is Life-giving.

The problem with meditation is that it is too simple for us. The difficulty for us – educated, specialized, sceptical and self-analytical as we are – is to accept its simplicity. It must be all the more difficult when we are badly educated, faddish and merely introspective. No doubt, it would be an easier teaching to communicate if it were complicated a little, if there were more of a psychological or intellectual apparatus. And, no doubt, there is a useful role for such interpretation of prayer, but in these talks the aim is an inducement to practice rather than to analysis. Conditioned as we are to seeing the questioning process as the way to truth, we – quite rightly – question anything claiming to be simple. Our conditioning, however, hinders us when it becomes a habit that controls us and prevents us from using that birthright of innocence which enables us to believe that simplicity does exist, can be communicated in a living tradition and deserves to be protected from complication.

So, if this book is introducing you to meditation for the first time, I do not ask you to believe at the outset that this is *the* way. But, because of the (I hope) simple approach of the book, I would ask you not to be suspicious of its message. We learn in the way we are taught and we pass on the message in the same way. John Main, as my teacher, is an exemplary model of simplicity and precision, as can be seen from his writings. I can understand that these qualities may at first be mistaken for exclusiveness or elitism: 'Are you saying meditation is *the only* way?' But as the years pass and the fruit of his teaching begins to appear right across the human and social spectrum, it becomes clear that to present meditation as the *fundamentally simple* way of prayer is an inclusive rather than exclusive approach. In the same sense, Christian missionary work has been transformed by remembering that Jesus' saying, 'I am the Way,' universalizes rather than limits his role as mediator. To say that following the riverbed will lead you to the sea does not exclude the river flowing over it, fed by many rivulets, or the fields and wildlife depending on the river. It is to state a simple fact, a fact that reveals simplicity in the overall design and direction of our Christian life.

To grow spiritually is to become less self-conscious and more simple. Progress in prayer cannot be measured except as we perceive a more pervasive spirit of love enter our daily life, as the Christian contemplative experience must bear fruit in the lives of others. The final word on how to pray is St Paul's first word on it – we do not even know how to pray, but the Spirit prays in us beyond all forms of language. Thus the guiding definition of Christian prayer is that *we* do not pray and that there are no methods of prayer. 'Our' prayer is our entering the prayer of Jesus, his Spirit which is the stream of love flowing between him and the Father.

To say what prayer is not raises necessary and illuminating questions about what prayer is. By way of introduction to this book I would like to look at three seminal questions that arise from the experience so many have already felt in their life as a result of 'discovering meditation' in the Christian tradition.

First, what is meditation? The word itself has acquired two meanings in Christian usage which, ironically, are almost contradictory. It is used here in its original sense, first introduced by the early monks from whose teaching *meditatio* has been given an attractive etymology as 'stare in medio' – to remain in the centre. *Meditari* was used to translate the Greek word *meletan*, which meant primarily to 'repeat'. Meditation was originally closely tied to the reading of Scripture by the desert monks as taught from master to disciple in a personal tradition. To *meditate* the Scriptures did not mean thinking or imagining them – this meaning came in much later and by way of 'spiritualities' that were not developed in the early centuries of Christianity. *Meditating* Scripture meant making it part of you through memorization and repetition. In order to focus the mind and heart of a disciple for the state of concentration, attention and interior silence necessary for prayer, a teacher would give him a single phrase or verse from Scripture. The monk would then repeat this phrase continuously, interiorly in his mind and heart and, in the words of John Cassian, one of the great teachers of the West, a teacher of St Benedict and St Thomas Aquinas, this repetition would cast out all 'riches of thought' and come to purity of heart by the 'poverty of this single verse'.[1]

This is the tradition we teach. Like any living tradition or doctrine, it has developed. It has not lost its simplicity but it has developed beyond the limits of the monastic–contemplative milieu and is being reappropriated as a birthright of every Christian. The use of such a repeated prayer-phrase can be seen in the apostolic Church, in the rabbinical teaching of Jesus' contemporaries, and in the teaching and practice of the New Testament Jesus himself. The Jesus-prayer of the Orthodox Church is evidently part of the same tradition.[2]

Why then does it strike us in the West as strange and foreign? Did we lose the tradition and if so, why? Evidently we did not lose it completely. *The Cloud of Unknowing*, an English fourteenth-century treatise, teaches the tradition but begins with the warning that it is a restricted teaching not meant for ordinary Christians. This warning is rightly understood by the thousands who buy paperback translations of the *Cloud* as an historical conditioning of a tradition that is trans-historical. Each rediscovery of the tradition represents an advance. The life of John Main witnesses to this.[3]

1. See A. de Vogüé, 'From John Cassian to John Main: Reflections on Christian Meditation', in *Monastic Studies*, xv, 1984.

2. See J. Main, *Monastic Prayer and Modern Man*, The Benedictine Priory of Montreal, 1981.

3. See L. Freeman, 'John Main's Monastic Adventure', in *Monastic Studies*, xv, 1984.

In 1954, John Main, as a practising Catholic, was taught meditation by a holy Indian teacher in Malaya. He was taught to repeat a single (Christian) phrase for the time of his meditation, two daily half-hours. He continued to worship and study in the Church and eventually was led to become a monk. When he described his way of 'meditation' to his novice master and where he had learnt it, he was told to stop. Under obedience, painfully but willingly accepted, he returned to the other more intellectual form of 'meditation' – discursive, conceptual and imaginative. He described this period of his life as his 'desert'.[4]

One day during a critical time in his life he reread John Cassian and, because of his previous experience of meditation, was able to recognize Cassian's *meditatio* as substantially identical with what he had learned from his Indian teacher. He had been led back onto his personal spiritual pilgrimage. And he was now uniquely situated to see the tradition as a universal one of great relevance and urgency both for Western society and for the Church that, through its own turmoil, was trying to lead all nations. John Main began to teach meditation in 1976 after a short stay at Thomas Merton's hermitage and three conferences to the monks of Gethsemani.[5] This led to the rapid, intense and yet powerfully purposeful mission of his last years, from the meditation centre at his monastery in London, to the new monastery he founded in Montreal and its now worldwide community of meditation groups.

What is the teaching? Sit down. Sit still. Close your eyes lightly. Sit relaxed but alert. Silently, interiorly begin to say a single word. We recommended the prayer-phrase, 'Maranatha.' Recite it as four syllables of equal length. Listen to it as you say it, gently but continuously. Do not think or imagine anything – spiritual or otherwise. If thoughts and images come, these are distractions at the time of meditation, so keep returning to the

---

4. J. Main, *The Gethsemani Talks*, The Benedictine Priory of Montreal, 1983.

5. *Ibid.*

simple work of saying the word. Meditate each morning and evening for between twenty and thirty minutes.

We call the prayer-word a 'mantra'. This is a Sanskrit term for what Cassian calls a 'formula' of prayer[6] and the *Cloud*, 'one little word'. The term 'mantra' has now entered English usage, just as the Hebrew 'amen' or the Greek 'Christos'. Perhaps this is a sign of the vast and mysterious process by which East and West are being married today.[7] But there is no special significance in its being an Eastern term. The advantage of using it is precisely that it does make us realize that this *meditation* is different from what we may think prayer to be. It is not about talking to God or thinking about God or asking for anything. The word 'maranatha' is Aramaic – Jesus' language – for 'Come, Lord'. It is one of the earliest recorded Christian prayers and was early used as what we would now call a mantra.[8]

The second question is, 'Why should I meditate?' Clearly, you will only meditate if *you* think you should, not because someone else does. In my experience of teaching meditation this is a question that does not need to be discussed by the people who do begin to follow the daily discipline of the 'way of the mantra'. However, that – for all that it tells us of the intuitive depth from which people hear and respond to the teaching – does not answer the question.

Motivation for starting to meditate depends on your starting point. It doesn't matter where you begin, for it is the same path, but at each stage of the pilgrimage there will be new ways of answering the question and so new depths of understanding. Many begin because as Christians they feel the urgent need to come to a deeper and more personal knowledge of their faith in Christ. Theology, worship, even works of charity are not ends in themselves. Nor, of course, are they just means. We

6. Cassian, *Conference* 10, ch. x.
7. See Bede Griffith's *The Marriage of East and West*. Collins, 1982; Fount Paperback, 1983.
8. 1 Cor. 16:22.

do not cease to theologize, worship or love each other when we start to meditate. But all these *point* – and the more faithfully they are done, the more relentlessly they point – to an interior reality of the *Person* of Christ. We need to know this Person whom we are serving, worshipping and talking about and we need to know him more and more fully, always more personally. Our knowledge of him is his love for us. Meditation is a Christian's way of loving him, our Lord, more wholly. To many Christians who begin to meditate at this point of consciousness in their journey, meditation represents something of the act of commitment that marriage or religious consecration signify in other dimensions of their life.

It would be absurd and presumptuous to say that meditation is only for the mature Christian. How can we humbly say 'mature' of ourselves, least of all about others? Many begin to meditate whose faith is weak or undeveloped and who are nominal Christians. A personal crisis or an unidentifiable anguish of the spirit straining beyond the superficiality and meaninglessness of modern life-styles can open the mind of anyone to the need to journey to the heart.

Finally, there are those of no faith or religious training. There will, in the years ahead, be an increasing number of these whom a numerically decreasing Church will have to address. Religious rituals and vocabulary will be increasingly ineffective means by themselves of sharing and communicating our faith unless there is a dimension of profound and experiential silence into which we can invite others to share the Presence with us.

Meditation is the way we respond to the call of Jesus to leave self behind. By silence of mind and spirit we are brought to that point of irreducible truth when we not only find ourselves but lose ourselves. The paschal mystery which Christ lives out humanly in us is the resolution of all the paradoxes of personal growth and human development that psychology, clinical or popular, put before us today. Meditation is a way of actual realization but not by means of self-improvement or self-analysis. To persevere on the pilgrimage is to have our motives progressively purified of self-interest. We come to see that for whatever reason we started to meditate, we meditate now because it is an essential part of the way we fulfil the destiny which the redemptive experience reveals. We meditate because we perish as full human beings if we do not find our spirit and the Spirit that is joined to our spirit.

Thirdly, why should we meditate *together*? The negative answer is clear enough whenever one meets with a religious community in the Church that has stopped praying together. As a spiritual community it has fallen apart, and the isolated, lonely lives of its individual members hold together with one another merely through social or professional bonds. Many orders and congregations that once received a hundred novices a year are now contemplating their extinction. Of course, whether we die individually or corporately, our death as Christians can be dignified by hope and bear witness to him for whom we live and die. But already while this is happening many new movements of religious community life are stirring, especially among the young whose search for community in a rootless and depersonalized culture has become a major priority. In this transition from one Christian era to another our perception of what went wrong in the old and what must be reaffirmed in the new is clearer every year: the depth of our community is directly proportionate to the depth of our prayer.

A common but deceptive feeling is that we can pray together only after we have come together at the other human levels of relationship. A simpler and the more truthful view is that a community of loving and mature people is created out of the prayer it enters together. The challenge of this in regard to meditation is evident. It asks us to be silent together, in faith, in the presence of the Spirit who *is* our unity. That is much to ask of people like ourselves who are products of media-consciousness. But until we can learn to be silently in communion with each other, we will have little to communicate. Again, it is a question of priorities, not of exclusion. We are not all meant to be hermits. But every Christian, every human being, is called to what we must perhaps find another word for in this context, the contemplative experience.

Religious communities are simply models of the Church. Whatever our vocation, every person naturally needs to belong to something that presents them with an ideal, that strengthens them to realize it and that gives them opportunities to transcend themselves. It is in answering this universal human need that the Church fulfils its mission to proclaim the gospel. When it tries to preach from a place where its members have failed to lead each other into a personal depth of experiencing the gospel, then its proclamation will fall flat. Lacking true authority, it will degenerate merely into exhortation or condemnation, defensive or aggressive authoritarianism.

Most people begin to meditate for largely personal reasons. It comes as a surprise to most to feel themselves drawn into a community which is essentially characterized not by news and views but by silence. What they thought to be most unshareable becomes the very thing that is most natural and necessary to share. There is usually a healthy, individualistic resistance to sharing it until one realizes that what is to be shared is nothing less than the Spirit which Jesus shares with each of us uniquely and personally, his self-giving. The Christian community that grows out of the silent depth of prayer does not need to be engineered. It grows. Of course, it is human and the laws of human association apply to it as elsewhere. But there is a quality that transcends law and that is the sure guarantee of the Church's ultimate survival: the spirit of liberty and love in which each of us is rebaptized at each time of prayer.

Such communities exert an influence in their social environment far beyond their numerical size. Most meditation groups, meeting in parishes, colleges, hospitals, or private homes are healthily small. They become centres of Presence and bring into being the new form of missionary endeavour that Western society now needs: a contemplative mission of Presence. As the meditators persevere on their personal pilgrimage, they find Christ's peace in the depth of their being to which the mantra is leading them. As we realize every month how precarious is the balance of power on which the world is resting, we must inform our work for peace with an experience of the real nature of peace. Christian meditation shows us peace as the energy of the Spirit of Christ and as a gift, not something gained by alternate force or political manoeuvrings. If we can release the peace already present in our hearts and if our communities can embody it, it will be a power nothing can stand against.

Unity and peace are inseparable aspects of spiritual growth. In the Church, as in most of our institutions, disunity and discord are presently the most evident characteristics. There will, let us hope, always be differences between groups and divergent opinions. But when differences become divisions, we can not hope to resolve them by argument alone. We need to remind ourselves in fact, not theory, of our underlying unity. The Word of God is not an opinion but the Truth to which all human minds aspire, some better than others, in a spirit of mutual correction and encouragement. The Word is enfleshed among us and within us. We must learn again to be silent and reverent in its presence. To learn to listen again we must first learn silence.

The talks in this book were given to weekly meditation groups meeting at the monastery in Montreal.[9] People of all ages, languages, backgrounds and opinions listened to them and then meditated for half an hour together. The groups that meet weekly in cities throughout the world similarly discover a tolerance and compassion from this experienced unity of spirit. There is no simpler proof of goodwill than to meditate with a person you disagree with. Capitalist and communist, conservative and liberal, black and white, male and female, Jew and Greek, Christian and Arab, Catholic and Protestant: there is a level of experience open to us all where these differences can cease to be divisions.

Simple can sound simplistic. Will all our problems be solved in Church and society at large if enough people meditate? The spiritual cannot be measured, and so there is no statistical correlation between what can happen in a group of ten and

9. As were those in J. Main, *Moment of Christ* (London and New York, 1984).

throughout a society. But in place of mathematical predictability we have access to the prophetic vision St Paul promised to those who are 'spiritual'. In this vision we can see the whole present in each of its parts – the holographic vision of the Body of Christ. What unfolds in each person unfolds in the community of which he is part. An ancient Chinese proverb expresses the hope of the Christian contemplative: one alone in silence who thinks the right thought changes the lives of thousands.

The fault in the simplistic approach is that it believes, or fools itself, that the correspondence of the part with the whole is an easy matter. The truthfulness of simplicity is that it sees and does not flinch from the difficulty of a path that must needs be narrow. Meditation is simple though not easy. But it is universally possible. It is as natural to the spirit as breathing is to the body.

An occasional objection to meditation is its apparent passivity. Experience of the mantra as spiritual *work* answers this. Nothing is less passive than the pure activity of being. We enjoy the human dignity of taking our destiny in our own hands when we learn how to accept the gift of our being.

All that we need to begin is faith and a sense of our vocation to be fully alive, to share in the very being of God. This vocation is not merely an option. It is written into our very being and we ignore it at the cost of our soul. Nothing is more urgent in our world than to discover this universal human vocation. The Spirit, coming to the aid of our weakness, is reminding us of it in many and diverse ways. In restoring us to this almost lost tradition, the Spirit is also showing us a way to fulfil that vocation.

LAURENCE FREEMAN

The Benedictine Priory of Montreal
June 1985, Feast of the Sacred Heart

The Light of the Word

When we talk or think about meditation, it is very easy to get carried away by theory. And meditation *is* an extremely exciting and wonderful mystery to talk and think about. But the talking and the thinking have a great inbuilt danger, which is that we do not go beyond the words and the ideas and instead remain looking at a reflection in a mirror. We are so fascinated by the reflection and so unaware that the mirror distorts whatever it reflects, that we fail to turn around and see the real thing.

The teaching of a great teacher like John Main has the power to inspire us to turn around and see the real thing. Seeing the real thing means *doing* the real thing. It means actually meditating, actually putting in the time, each morning and evening, to see the real thing. The teaching we have received, which we try to share and to live, is entirely realistic and practical. It is not concerned just with speculation or elaborating theories; it is concerned primarily with experience, experience in faith. First, it is concerned with the experience we all start from as we begin to meditate. Secondly, it is concerned with the experience we pass through as we learn to meditate. Only thirdly is it concerned with the experience we enter into, the goal we arrive at. Because of that intimate connection between the teaching and our own experience, the teaching itself has the authority to reflect and guide our experience. This is what we call a 'living tradition'.

Each of us enters into it when we begin to meditate. Because it is a tradition that began a long time ago, it is one that has to a great degree formed us into who we are when we come to enter it. That teaching, that tradition, is simplicity itself. It says that to meditate we have to become silent and still, not just externally, not just physically – though those are essential dimensions – but interiorly silent, interiorly still. In this way the tradition leads us to enter the knowledge of unity with ourselves. The teaching leads us to find ourselves. Our exterior stillness reflects the interior stillness. When we meditate we must try to sit as still as possible and not get careless about this discipline of stillness as the weeks and months pass. It may seem a very elementary thing to do but it is the first step, and the first step is all-important. Then you begin to say your mantra. During the time of your meditation you have nothing else to do, nothing else to worry about, nothing to be ambitious about, to plan or to analyse. You have only to say your word. Saying your word will lead you into the ever profounder silence in which you find you can be who you are and (even more wonderful) allow God to be who God is within you.

Whatever thoughts, ideas or images may float across your mind, just let them float away. Whatever great insights may come to you, just let them go too. Whatever trivial thoughts or distractions may come to you, just let them go. It doesn't matter what comes into your mind or what you imagine; simply return to the saying of your word. Repetition purifies. The mantra will purify your heart, your consciousness, and bring you to that pure simplicity of a child which we need if we are going to enter the Kingdom. The mantra is the *way*. When most of us begin the way, our initial experience is very different from what we are eventually led to. It is not one of joy, peace and contentment. We hear this teaching of how to live out of the spring of joy within us. We set out to find the realm of peace within us. Probably, to begin with, we are more likely to encounter restless desire and discontentment. We are all radically discontented because we are encouraged and trained to live so much in the future, planning for the future, or in the past, regretting or analysing it over and over again. Our restlessness makes us miss the only opportunity we have for contentment, for fullness of life. The only chance we have is the present moment. Missing that we miss everything.

Living in the past or the future we end up discontented, because in being so concerned about what we lack, so preoccupied with what we desire, we fail to see what we have been given. Unless we change this attitude and turn around from the mirror, we are condemned to being discontented. Even when we do get what we desire from time to time, we will still be discontented. Getting what we desire will not satisfy us, because in that concupiscent frame of mind there will always be something else to want beyond our immediate reach. The state of discontent is ruled not by the spirit of love but by egoism. The only way into peace is to recognize and receive what we have been given. The greatest gift that we have been given usually misses our attention. We usually fail to see it. It is not health, wealth, beauty or talent. The greatest gift is our being, simply the fact that we *are*. This is the first and fundamental gift. If we fail to recognize that, which also means failure to accept it, then nothing that comes our way will really become ours either. Accepting that gift is the first step, the essential step to becoming fully alive and therefore fully content.

Accepting the gift is what we do when we meditate. Meditation is concerned with being rather than with doing, although this is something it takes us a long time to become familiar with as an idea and even longer to accept as an experience. It is very difficult for us to be concerned with being rather than with doing. For a while, after we begin to meditate we still regard our meditation as being concerned primarily with doing. We have to recognize this as how we begin. But our perception is purified as we continue. As we learn how to be, how to accept the gift of our being, we find real contentment. We leave behind desire, restlessness and all the images that those passions create. As a result, of course, our *doing* is itself radically purified by our meditation. The way we live, the quality of our life, the generosity of our relationships, are all in time transformed by the new understanding we learn by learning to be and by accepting the gift of our being.

All that is a process of growth in our spirit. It is not an instant experience. That is why when we begin to meditate it is important not to look for experiences, certainly not to try to engineer or simulate them, to anticipate or possess them. It is a process of growth which is similar to the gradual settling of the impurities in a glass of water. At first all the impurities swirl around making the water cloudy, opaque. But if you don't interfere with the glass and if you allow it to stand still and the impurities to settle, the water itself becomes still and so translucently clear. As you look through the water you realize how beautiful is its purity, its clarity and you see what simplicity really is. When it is opaque the water reflects. When it is clear you see through it.

The first thing we have to learn to do is to allow ourselves to settle, to be still. We are all of us cloudy. We are all too self-reflective. We have to allow our consciousness to become clarified. This is the simplifying process of meditation, becoming still at the pure centre of our being. This means really still, not just thinking about being still or saying how nice it would be if we were still and more spiritual, but in fact being still and in time allowing all our action to flow from harmony with that stillness. In stillness our spirit clarifies. It becomes pure and translucent. The God whose Spirit dwells within us then shines through our spirit as sunlight shines through the water. This is what we call purity of heart. This is the clarity of consciousness that allows us to see God. 'Blessed are the pure of heart,' said Jesus, 'for they shall see God.'

Kierkegaard defined purity of heart as desiring one thing. Most of us desire too many things. Restricting our desire to one thing gradually purifies us of desire. It clarifies us, because when we meditate all we desire is to say our mantra. Everything else is left behind. Saying our word faithfully, simply and lovingly, brings us to that stillness where we see the light clearly both within and around us. Therefore we see everything clearly because we see it in the light which is the very medium of vision. The psalmist praised God by singing: 'In your light we see light.'

This clarity is felt as joy. Seeing the light is the essence of joy and so it is the only secure basis of contentment in our life.

As the spirit of peace it works for tranquillity and harmony in every area of life. It is only necessary that we do become still, then that we stay on the path that leads us further into the stillness. The path only asks us to be totally simple at those two periods of meditation each day and to be as faithful as we can to the saying of our word.

The Light we find is the light of the Word described in the Gospel of John:

> When all things began, the Word already was. The Word dwelt with God, and what God was the Word was. The Word, then, was with God at the beginning, and through him all things came to be; no single thing was created without him. All that came to be was alive with his life, and that life was the Light of men. The light shines on in the dark, and the darkness has never mastered it. (John 1:1–5)

Total Transformation

If there seems to be an absolute quality about the way of meditation, it is because the call of the Gospel itself is absolute. Our meditation is essentially a response to the direct summons of the Gospel to leave self behind. It is heard by each one of us personally and uniquely because the Spirit of Jesus which makes the call felt, dwells within the heart of each person uniquely. The uniqueness of personhood is an absolute reality. The fundamental call of the Gospel is to conversion, a turning from ourselves to the One who calls. Turning means precisely what it says, changing direction from our hopes and fears, turning away from the past and the future and, ultimately, to turn from our very self-consciousness.

It is a call from and to the roots of our being. The Gospel expresses it very simply and starkly as a call to die. Conversion is a process of spiritual growth by which we die to our own selves. We die when we enter into a death, which for a Christian is the dying of Jesus, so that we may be at one with him in his resurrection. This image of turning which expresses the call to conversion is drawn from a simple physical example of something turning around – a solid body turning around in space. When we feel a little overchallenged by the absolute nature of the call we should think of the implications of the metaphor. It is an absolute call but it allows for a *progressive* turning. It does not expect a complete turn around in one go. Although we are all called to turn completely round a full 360°, we achieve this goal most probably by doing it a half degree at a time, or perhaps a tenth of a degree at a time. To consider the absolute nature of the call requires a realistic understanding of the progressive nature of the conversion process. It is an on-going conversion, an on-going transformation of consciousness. As a growth process the transformation becomes progressively real for us through our fidelity to the pilgrimage of meditation – an on-going commitment every morning and every evening. Our commitment to conversion is a commitment to growth and one that we make real and incarnate in our twice-daily meditation.

I recently spoke to some people who were very opposed to meditation. They were opposed to teaching it because, they said, it seemed too simple. 'You are making too big a claim by saying, "Just say the mantra and everything will happen automatically." It is not like that, and if you think that it is then you are fooling yourself.' It is a difficult statement to answer, because unless you are willing to enter into the experience of meditation you won't know how realistic it is. It is difficult to transmit, for example, how the saying of our mantra reinforces our commitment to the conversion experience of the Gospel in every part of our life, in every relationship, in every project we undertake, in every work we do. It is difficult to suggest how the saying of the mantra commits us to the progressive loss of self and to the on-going experience of conversion in ordinary life. And it is even more difficult to express the growing intuition that, in fact, perseverance in saying the mantra gives us the power to make a personal commitment to the reality of the Kingdom. Nonetheless it is *absolutely* true that *simply* saying the mantra commits us to living out the consequences of saying the mantra.

This is perhaps the way to see into an essential truth of the Gospel. By it we know and feel that the spiritual reality of our meditation transforms the moral reality of our life. The moral reality of our life begins to mature because we are impelled to be truthful to the implications of saying the mantra in every level of life. We can't meditate every day and continue to pursue a policy of deception, of self-interest, of revenge. However gradually, we must also begin to commit ourselves in daily life to truthfulness, to love, to God. This is why it is our spiritual life which transforms our world. As our moral integrity begins to develop, our actions will inevitably begin to change and so the reality of the world we live in, the world of social, political or religious beings, begins to change as well. The core of John Main's teaching is that we must first learn to be and then we will know what to do. *Ama et fac quod vis* (The power to do good comes from being good). What we *do* is only changed deeply and permanently by what we *are*. This is a way of saying that Christ is simultaneously present in our hearts, in our worship and in our world. There is one Christ whose energy of love fuels the all-embracing work of transformation, of conversion. Our part is to grasp and be faithful to the truth that it is the awakening of our consciousness to his indwelling Spirit that triggers the consciousness of the world. The Church teaches as a leaven, by influence, not by force.

So, by our conversion we arrive at mindfulness of the one Christ present in our hearts and in the world, not remembering Jesus by turning our imagination to the past ('We no longer know Christ after the flesh' (2 Cor. 5:16)) but mindful of his presence in the present moment. And it is the mantra that anchors us in the present moment. This mindfulness is Christian enlightenment: illumination by the mind of Christ, by his consciousness which has been transfigured into pure love, by the light of divine love. We awaken to this presence at the deepest level of consciousness. It takes time for it to break the surface of our consciousness but as it rises to the surface, as the light begins to spread through our consciousness, so the depth of our mindfulness grows. And that is our entry into the all-pervading consciousness of the risen Christ.

This is from the Letter to the Romans:

If we have become incorporate with him in a death like his, we shall also be one with him in a resurrection like his. We know that the man we once were has been crucified with Christ . . . But if we thus died with Christ, we believe that we shall also come to life with him. We know that Christ, once raised from the dead, is never to die again: he is no longer under the dominion of death. For in dying as he died, he died to sin, once for all, and in living as he lives, he lives to God. In the same way you must regard yourselves as dead to sin and alive to God, in union with Christ Jesus. (Rom. 6:5–6, 8–11)

How Long?

When we begin to meditate we inevitably want to know, 'How long will it take?' That question occurs so automatically to our minds that it is important to come to terms with it. And we have to find out how to approach the question, as we are all likely to feel somewhat discouraged as we make the inner pilgrimage. Beginning to meditate is much like setting out on a journey. You set out because you want to leave where you are and you want to get somewhere, and so at the outset you are full of enthusiasm. Halfway along the journey you often get tired. At different points along the way, if you get delayed or the going gets rough, you may become discouraged. Then you say, 'Well, should I continue? Is it worth it?' That kind of question takes many forms. 'Am I really the kind of person to meditate?' 'Is this for me?' Or, 'Why don't I feel as if I am making progress?' Maybe somebody close to you will then tell you, 'You know, you are a great deal easier to live with now than you were six months or a year ago.' But you may not *feel* as if you are particularly better. 'Why don't I feel it?' we ask.

These kinds of questions are serious opportunities of growth on the journey, rather like making plane connections, changing trains or buses. We have to confront them but without wasting too much time on them. We must not forget that it *is* a journey and we have to keep moving. Self-analysis is a way of stopping, getting off the bus, breaking the journey and missing the connection. Of course these kinds of feelings or questions are not continuous. They are only moods we pass through and, as we become more clarified, we come to see that they are moods of the ego. Although it is the ego we are travelling away from, it is like a shadow that stays with us and every so often, as we change direction, the shadow is cast in front of us and we feel ourselves 'in the shadow'. Those moods try to persuade us to give up. If we learn how to go through them, they progressively decrease. And even if they do return from time to time, they do so with less and less power. The darkness of the shadow diminishes as the sun gets higher in the sky.

Why is that question, 'How long will it take?' so important and how can it be so discouraging? Partly because it is such an unclear question. It is a question that we need to ask, but after all what does it mean? How long will *what* take? What is it that meditation is trying to make happen? What is the goal? What is the destination? Meditation will certainly lead us into an ever-deeper encounter with our own reality, and because of that it will give our life a more stable dimension of peace, liberty of spirit and joyfulness of heart. And we will begin to feel those new dimensions opening up from within and, in our lives, often from quite unexpected sources, in unexplored relationships, at unpredicted moments, at unmarked points. These new spiritual dimensions exert a perceptible influence upon our relationships and work, our way of responding to the decisions and challenges of each day. What happens is that a whole set of forces, inter-connected in the unity of our spirit, is released in our centre and radiates outwards to our lives. But it is not even this that is the fundamental goal. It isn't this we are asking about when we say, 'When will *it* happen?' All these real and necessary dimensions, all these inter-dependent forces are signs and symbols of one unified force, the one unified reality. This is the power of the reality of the Spirit of God who dwells in our heart, in the final depth of our spirit, the Spirit of all creation which is also the ultimate goal and meaning of our life. 'How long will *it* take? When will *it* happen?' When we understand that 'it' is this Spirit in our hearts that we are talking about and trying somehow to express, we will approach these questions quite differently. Because we then know that 'it' is the Spirit which is both the beginning and the end, the alpha and omega. It is the beginning and the end of our meditation, of the whole journey of our meditation taken from the day we begin until the last day of our life. It is this Spirit which initiates and completes our being. As we come to understand that as the answer, we come to understand our questions. 'How long does it take?' It takes *no time* because that Spirit is eternal and all time is contained in that Spirit. 'When will it happen?' It has *already* happened. The Spirit has already been breathed into our hearts.

What we are really asking is how long will it take us to follow the absolutely simple path of meditation with an absolute simplicity of spirit. In a certain sense, that is entirely up to us. In a real sense, *we* decide how long it will take. How long will it be before we commit ourselves to the simplicity of that Spirit, to the simplicity of that Truth. It *is* totally simple only because it is fundamental. Everything else is built on it. How long will it take us to commit ourselves to it totally? It usually takes us so long (and much longer than it need) just because we keep forgetting how to be simple, how to be committed. We remember to be simple, and so progressively committed, by saying the mantra. Saying it we are rooted in and nourished by the simplicity and commitment of Christ. Saying the mantra is our fundamental state of simplicity. We become complex only when we begin to think about ourselves, to ask self-referring questions. 'How long will it take *me*?' Any question that has 'I' or 'me' in it automatically becomes complex. But in saying the mantra, we are not questioning or thinking about ourselves. Or at least we are committed to moving beyond thinking about ourselves. The first step in simplicity is to say the mantra. And because we can so easily forget that fundamental simplicity, it is important to remind each other of the unremitting simplicity of the way.

Taking the time to meditate often means making a real sacrifice of time in busy lives that are full of responsibilities. But simplicity asks us to offer the sacrifice of half an hour of precious time each morning and evening and to find a place and time that is as quiet as possible, ideally at early morning and early evening. If you can, choose the same place for each

Light Within

meditation. That will help you to establish a rhythm and pattern in your life. You won't then find it so much of a melodrama to make that sacrifice each day. It will become an inbuilt part of your life. But if you can't find the same time and the same place, set aside the two periods anyway. Then, at those times determine to be silent, learn to be still. Try to sit as still as you can. Take a few moments to find a position you will be able to remain in as comfortably as you can for the whole meditation. The only basic rule of how to sit is to keep your back straight. Then silently, interiorly, begin to say your word, your mantra. The mantra we recommend you to say is the word, 'Maranatha'. Say it as four syllables of equal length, 'ma-ra-na-tha'. Say it from the beginning of your meditation continuously right through to the end. That is all we have to do. What could be simpler?

One of the first things we discover is that it is not easy to be simple but that difficulty presents us with something of an exciting challenge. Sit down, sit still and say your mantra: difficult, yes, but possible because simple.

What we are really asking when we say, 'How long?' is 'How long will enlightenment take?' We tend to say, 'Can I do it?' 'Is it for me?' 'Aren't I too busy?' or 'too artistic?' or 'too exuberant?' '. . . too imaginative?' Or we say, 'Aren't I too unworthy? Aren't I too egotistical? Aren't I too selfish? . . . too self-conscious? I am all these things. And therefore, I can't meditate.' What we are asking is, 'Am I too human to be enlightened?' To answer that question we need the faith to begin to meditate. By beginning we learn pretty quickly that we meditate as disciples, not as entrepreneurs. We are disciples of the Spirit, not exploiters of the Spirit. The disciple enters into the enlightenment of his Master because there is only the one enlightenment. As disciples of Jesus (because it is his Spirit that lives in our hearts) we know in faith that it is his enlightenment that shines in our hearts, the light of his awakened consciousness. And we know that it shines in every human heart. It shines in every heart *because* we are human, not in spite of our humanity.

The only question is 'How long does it take us to open our eyes to his light, to open the eye of our heart, our consciousness to his?' Even with our physical eyes closed we can know if there is light around us. Similarly, however dimly, at this very moment, we each know that we are enlightened. We know it because Jesus knows it in us. It is his Spirit's self-knowledge within us. *It* only takes us as long as it takes us to understand *that*. Becoming simple means becoming centred no longer in ourselves but in him. Learning to say the mantra simply means learning to take the attention off ourselves. To let go not only of that self-referring question but of all questions and of all self-centred concerns. We do so with a minimum of effort because the way is the way of simplicity of heart and gentleness of spirit. We say the mantra continuously but we say it gently. Use only enough effort to say it. It isn't a weapon. It is a harmonic that we sound. Say it gently and then you will learn to say it with love. To be in harmony is to be in love with all.

Consider these words about the enlightenment of Jesus in the Letter to the Ephesians:

Everything, when once the light has shone it up, is illumined. And everything thus illumined is all light. And so the hymn says: 'Awake, sleeper, rise from the dead, and Christ will shine upon you'. (Eph. 5:13–14)

Thought and Feeling

I suppose if a meditator were to have an ideal it would be complete other-centredness. Christian idealism is always eminently realistic and optimistic. It understands that the ideal is attainable but something that we grow into. We understand too that humanly this ideal is attainable because it has been attained by Jesus and that we share in his achievement. For us to be holy, which is our destiny, is simply to share fully in his holiness. And as we progress on that path of union into Christ we come to understand in an ever fuller and richer consciousness what it means to be other-centred in *him*. We understand that the way of other-centredness is a way that can be followed only as a way of wholeness, and so as we become integrated persons we will, even to our surprise, become more other-centred. To be holy, to be whole, is another way of saying that we are turned towards the other. We cannot be whole without another. This is the way of goodness. So we discover that everything in us has to be involved in our Christian transformation and many of the divisions and internal contradictions that exist within us have to be left behind. We must have the courage to let go of our compartmentalized selves and become simple.

We understand this perhaps most immediately and ordinarily in terms of the great split we make in ourselves between intellect and feeling. It would be difficult for most of us to say which controls us most of the time: our intellect or our emotions. We would like to think that we act rationally and that our minds are in control of our emotions, but probably most of the time our emotions exert the stronger pull. Our rational perception of life is often coloured by our moods, optimistic now, down-hearted a few hours later.

One of the refreshing dimensions of freedom which meditation brings, gradually and perhaps painfully, is a liberty of spirit which opens up the freedom from being dominated by our emotions; this is a freedom gained in large measure by the discipline of our meditation because we meditate *whatever* we feel like, indeed whether we feel like meditating or not. What we may feel during the meditation does not affect our fidelity to the discipline of the mantra. But this is not, as one might think, a way of crushing the feelings of our emotional life. Meditation isn't a way of non-feeling any more than it is anti-intellectual; it is a way of wholeness. No part of us can be repressed, rejected or left outside of the Kingdom and in fact, as we probably come to experience after a year or two of meditation, our emotional sensitivity will more likely increase as a result of that discipline. We will probably be more vulnerable. There will be fewer ways of evasion or of self-deception, fewer escape routes for the ego and still less as we go on. So it isn't that we stop feeling any more than we stop thinking. We don't use our thinking faculties during meditation but we will probably discover that our thinking, our power of thought and rational perception is clarified and focused as the result of meditation. In the same way our emotional faculty is harmonized, stabilized. Exactly how this occurs is probably impossible to analyse by the very nature of wholeness. It is the given mystery of the path we are following.

What is happening is that we are being unified, which means that the different dimensions of our being are gradually being brought into synchrony, into harmony, into step with each other. While they work against each other, or even while they work separately from each other, we are in a state of complexity – and we all know the anxiety, the dis-ease and sense of apprehension which is a result of our humanity being dislocated and fractured into complexity. But when they function together, when they merge into each other and co-operate in harmony, we experience peace, well-being and a capacity to be generous with ourselves. The more we thus come into possession of ourselves the easier it is to practise dispossession of ourselves. All these different parts of our being come together under the guiding influence of a power that transcends both thinking and feeling and unites them both at a higher level of consciousness. This is the power of the Spirit. Meditation is the way to be fully open to the power of the Spirit which is the power of the Spirit of Christ united in love to our spirit.

So during the times of meditation we are not primarily functioning through thought or feeling. But we are penetrating the reality of our *spirit* which involves us inevitably with the reality of Christ. We cannot find our own spirit without finding Christ. Our thinking and feeling powers obviously remain with us. We pick them up again after each meditation, and we can hope to use them more clearly, more generously as a result of their being purified by silence. They remain with us but, as it were, as a silent non-interfering companion on the spiritual journey. They accompany us into the depths of our spiritual identity and are there transformed. This is the work of wholeness, of integration. It is the work of being prepared for the entry into the Kingdom, the Kingdom which it is possible for us to enter only when we are in the childlike state of wholeness.

We cannot leave anything behind. This work of integration is the work of sanctification. Holiness is a vital reality for us as Christians to understand and not to be embarrassed by. Holiness is essentially a quality of being. It is the way we are. It is not, as we often think, just the merited result of what we do. Yet a specific characteristic of Christian holiness is the quality of our action. So what we do is vitally involved in the Christian life in the journey of meditation. Again, one doesn't have to be on the journey for very long before one discovers that meditation is changing both the *way* we do things and, in crucial moments of decision, *what* we do.

What we do is a sure sign of who we are, where we are. And what we do is also a vital way of realizing who we are. This is why the sign of holiness is love and why our progress in meditation, in all spiritual growth, is a growth in other-centredness.

It is evident both in the way we think and in the way we feel, in the changes, the transformation of mind and heart which is the Christian experience. Our thinking is changed because our thought will become less and less occupied with ourselves. We will be less preoccupied with self-analysis as we become holier, more whole. Most of the time we turn the light of reason upon ourselves, examining, measuring, analysing, anticipating what concerns *me*. But as the consciousness of Christ expands within our consciousness we will instead turn the light of reason away from self into his mystery and into a perception and penetration of the presence of God, of the divine dimension in every aspect of life, in creation. The result of this will be the new dimension of peace that is the fruit of the Christian transformation. Self-analysis produces anxiety, but our thought turned beyond ideas, like our vision purified of images, approaches the mystery of God in self-transcending wonder.

And emotionally too, we will experience our feelings more sympathetically, which means that we won't simply be feeling in order to explore ourselves, our own states of consciousness or our own moods, but we will use the emotional faculty in order to enter into the experience of others. Our feelings will be less and less turned in upon themselves (feeling what we feel) and more lovingly turned towards others, so that we can feel with them, feel for them, and even feel in them. This other-centredness of the Christian life to which all are called is the fruit of a consciousness higher than self-consciousness. We know in the full light of Christian revelation that this is the consciousness of Christ, his human consciousness, totally other-centred. His mind and his heart are wholly turned from self to the Father and to us.

This is from the letter to the Colossians. St Paul is talking about the task assigned to him:

to deliver [God's] message in full; to announce the secret hidden for long ages and through many generations, but now disclosed to God's people, to whom it was his will to make it known – to make known how rich and glorious it is among

all nations. The secret is this: Christ in you, the hope of a
glory to come.

Trans-Formation

At the core of the Gospel is the invitation to be changed, made
into a new form, and it is the experience of that transformation
which gives the writings of the New Testament their power.
This is how John Main talks about it in *Word into Silence*.
He has just quoted a favourite passage from Romans: 'Adapt
yourselves no longer to the pattern of this present world but
let your minds be remade and your whole nature thus transformed.' He goes on to say that this transformation of our
nature is put before us as a real and immediate possibility. It
is also the essential Christian experience of being born again
in the Holy Spirit. Being born again happens as we realize the
power of the living Spirit of God within us.

Realizing this is the path of meditation, which is therefore a
way of transformation and rebirth. Every time we sit down to
meditate we are changed. We are never quite the same after-
wards. Every time we meditate we undergo *renewal*, which is
another word to describe in the New Testament that experience
of transformation, shedding old-ness and being made new. So
the invitation of the Gospel addresses itself to a very deeply
felt need in the human heart, the need we all have, regardless
of our religious faith or of our spiritual maturity, but simply as
human beings to be changed. Involved in this felt need is the
intuition that we have to be born again if the very meaning of
our conception and birth is to become fully conscious. We all
know that we have to change, because we cannot grow without
changing and you cannot really be alive in any meaningful or
certainly any enjoyable sense unless you are growing. To grow

means both to go forward into the unknown and obviously, therefore, to leave the past behind.

Although we have this deeply rooted intuition of the need to change, to be transformed, we also fear it because it is a part of the package of human nature to resist the unknown. Instead of letting go of the past we hang on to it, even when it is the very thing that we want to shed. So we often hang on to the most painful, anxious or uncreative remnants of the past. These in various forms we call neuroses or fixations or obsessions. All the psychological apparatus of our own time is really concerned with that inherent tendency of the human mind and heart to resist the movement of the human mystery to go beyond itself, to resist the forces of growth because of the fear of losing self. The danger of pursuing a psychological rather than spiritual path is, therefore, of failing to grow and staying put in mere self-fascination, looking into an ever-increasing maze of mirrors, at a finite amount of experience, the old-ness of the past which stifles renewal.

We need only reflect on the words of Jesus to understand what we are created for, 'Leave self behind'. We are created to let go of the past and that means accepting the challenge, which we find the most radical of all, to forget the past. We fear forgetting the past, we resist living fully in the present and so we find it difficult to say the mantra. But if we can learn courageously, with faith, how to forget the past, then in that loss of self we move forward. What moves forward is the whole person we have become up to that point in time and thus the whole past is no longer merely present as a memory to fascinate or indulge our self-preoccupation, but it becomes integrated into the wholeness of the personal mystery that we are called onward to be. We need to forget the past in order for it to be wholly absorbed in the present.

So in the light of the teaching of Jesus we lose self in order to find self, and by losing self we are transformed. What we are changed into is not, as we fear, something other than what we are. We fear that if we lose ourself we will become another, something else. One of the most powerful and fearful symbols in every mythology is the transformation of one creature into another. And it is what we all fear might happen if we forget ourselves. But it is a fear that is totally cast out of our hearts when we open them to the love of God that has flooded us through the Spirit of Christ who dwells in our heart. Love teaches us that we are changed simply into who we are, that the transformation is becoming the person we are. There *is* loss but loss only of form; a trans-formation. We pass from one form to another on the particular pilgrimage that each of us follows, and the transformation is achieved by being open to what lies beyond form, to the essence of the person we are, which means to our spirit. In the deepest interiority of our spirit, we find the Spirit of God, present to us in the loving Spirit of Jesus. In the heart of the humanity which we fear to lose we find the humanity of Jesus transformed by his utter openness to God.

It is a way of wonder and ordinariness. On the way we encounter many problems – problems from the past, problems of integration, problems of adaptation, problems of facing the future. It seems to us that in order to solve the problems thrown up by the process of transformation we have to discover ways of bringing solutions in from outside, to acquire information, to increase knowledge and discover new techniques. The teaching of the Gospel is that our problems *are* solved, and we need not be trying to complicate our ways of dealing with them but should rather be learning to be poor. Poverty confronts our resistance to change more effectively than any mere 'solution'.

So the way to solve our problems and to meet the challenges on the Christian path of transformation is not self-analysis, not going out of ourselves looking for solutions. Rather it is the way of poverty which is the dynamic of our meditation. Any transformation that occurs through that poverty transforms not only ourselves but the problems themselves. So often we are the problem. It is that experience of the transcendence of our own problems that we are invited to see in the miracle stories of the Gospel.

We find this in community life, which gives a special vividness and immediacy through the experience of sharing. We discover that the teaching of the Gospel, of the community we share, of our spiritual tradition takes many forms and incarnations. In the apparently restricted and narrow life of community there is the most amazing expansion, the most wonderful variety of forms. Living a common life teaches us to be open to the Spirit who is not restricted by any form but who can take any form and is living through all forms – bringing them into the one form that endures, the one image that does not change, which is Christ. In loving each other, which is the Christian way of problem-solving, we find Christ, who is the supreme resolution of the human dilemma. The power to love and so to make this discovery is the goal of our meditation.

The Plough

The actual practice of meditation takes us beyond images. It is pure prayer, and through it we enter into the reality that images only point towards. It is an extraordinary discovery that we can do that. The images and also the symbols that images point towards are important to us in life to prepare us to meditate: how would we know about it otherwise? They deepen our understanding and therefore our personal integration for the journey beyond images. The important thing is to perceive the preparatory image and then act upon it by going beyond it. The distractions we have in meditation are images thrown up by the journey, and at first when we set out the distractions are so powerful that they stop us at almost every step on the way. We take two steps and then we're knocked over by an avalanche of distractions and we have to start again and again. That faithful return is always going to be demanded of us, but as we go on there comes a dimension of the journey (and the journey is always opening up into new dimensions) when the distractions may be there but they become less potent, less capable of actually stopping us from walking the path.

This is what lies behind what Father John (in *Word into Silence*) calls the second preliminary aim of meditation. 'The second aim is to say the mantra throughout the meditation without interruption while remaining calm in the face of all distraction. In this phase the mantra resembles a plough that continues resolutely across the rough fields of our mind undeflected by any obtrusion or disturbance.' That image of the plough drawn from the Gospel is a powerful aid to us to understand what the journey is and what the saying of the mantra does.

It is not meant as an image for us to take into our meditation, to think about the mantra as a plough as we say it. But it is meant, as are the parables of Jesus, to give us the clarity of understanding we need to make a free, mature and personal commitment to the journey. And we need clarity and depth of understanding if our response is going to be as fully personal as it is meant to be. The mantra as the plough helps us to understand that the opening of our heart (which is the purpose of prayer) is the preparation, the furrowing, the clearing of the ground. It is preparing the ground for the next stage which is the dropping of the seed.

The dropping of the seed leads then to the unfolding of natural energies of growth, the spiritual energies of love and the life of Christ, working deep within us.

Remember the parable of the Kingdom where the man buries the treasure that he has found and goes off to sell everything. We are continually burying the seed deep in our heart, dropping it into the depth that the plough has opened up. We are not trying to watch it grow. Indeed we cannot watch it grow. The Kingdom cannot be observed, because it cannot be self-conscious. The pure consciousness of the Kingdom is found beyond self-consciousness. So we are continually opening the ground, dropping the seed, and allowing it to fall into the silence. We let go of our curiosity, of our desire to control, possess and monitor. Above all, we let go of the seductive temptation to be fascinated with what is going on within ourselves. If we really want to grow we have to let go of our self-fascination and lose ourselves in pure wonder. The plough perseveres across the field.

Ideally, it follows a direct line. There are no short-cuts on the spiritual path. But meditation *is* a direct path and it is a great gift given to us to proclaim and to share with everyone as a route without diversions. It is easier to wander, to leave the highways and get lost on the back roads. But it becomes more and more frustrating. In the words of Jesus, when you

have put your hand to the plough and if you want to be really
of the Kingdom, do not look back. That is the fidelity in saying
the mantra continuously, the trust not to look back to see what
is happening, where it has gone, whether the seed fell in the
place that you thought it would fall: the faith to look constantly
ahead – not fascinated by past experiences, nor trying to
analyse what happened last week or in childhood, but letting
go of self-consciousness in the poverty of looking directly
ahead. We let go of the past and are rooted in the present. In
the fidelity of the daily return we unite past and future in the
present moment of Christ.

And where is Christ in all this? He is everywhere in it. He
is in the ground, the ground of our being. He is in the plough.
He is in the growth of the seed. He is in the silence. And he
is in the yoke that we accept, that we need, the yoke of discipline for us to stay in contact with the plough. He is present
in every aspect of life, and our meditation opens us to know
him not as an idea or a symbol, not even as an ideal, but as a
person present in everything that we are. Our meditation opens
up to the dimension where he is, and we find that everything
we truly are is in that dimension too. How do we meet him?
The encounter with Jesus is the summons of our discipleship.
We meet him by seeking him in faith. We love him before we
see him. That is the silence of our faith. And also the faith by
which we become silent. We cannot meet him separate from
him because he is in us and we in him by union.

That meeting is the unfolding of our vocation. It is the
unfolding of our own personhood. It is the unfolding of the
Kingdom. We meet him not only in meditation. We meet him
in others. That is the power and the meaning of the Christian
community, because we can only realize that union by turning
away from our own separateness. Self-fascination is a commitment to separateness, to isolation. Turning away from that –
and that is what a community enables us to do – we discover
we can commit ourselves to something beyond it, to the reality
of an existing union. And so we turn away from self-fascination
and all the sadness it brings and turn instead, with the help of

each other's example, each other's silence, fidelity and perseverance, to the wonder and peace of being together in Jesus who is the bond between us.

Choosing Life

Meditation is about discovering fullness of life and therefore becoming fully alive. The key word of the first three Gospels is the *Kingdom* and the key word of the Gospel of John is *Life*. Kingdom and Life because the Kingdom *is* the fullness of Life. Meditation is the way into the Kingdom because it is the way to become fully alive. John Main described meditation as the way fully to accept the gift of our being. What we have to discover – and we can only discover it by perseverance – is that our being can only become alive when we do actually accept it. There is existence and there is life. Existence is something we have to break out of, and when we break out of it we break into life. Existence is bounded on all sides; there are limits. But in life there is no limit; life is eternal. We have to find a way to convert existence into life, to move beyond and through the boundaries which are simply the boundaries of our own egoism, of our fear of life and of expanding beyond ourselves.

Each of us at this moment has a problem in life. For some of us perhaps that problem or cluster of problems is latent and for some extreme. To leave self behind means leaving those problems behind. It means leaving those deep concerns because they are not ultimate, because they exist only within the boundaries of our limitations. We are much fonder of our problems, things that limit us, than we might think, much more attached to the pains and the crosses we carry than we need be.

It seems to us that we cannot let them go, that we carry them with us wherever we go. But when we step across the boundaries we do let them go and we discover that our life is not restricted by those boundaries any more than our capacity to be alive is ultimately restricted by our problems. But to make that step requires courage. In the simplest terms it is the courage to be, the courage to accept the gift. It seems absurd that we should need courage to accept a gift, and yet it is understandable because in accepting the gift we lose ourselves. By accepting the gift of being we transcend ourselves.

This sounds very obvious and it is. But it is something that the confusion of being limited, the complexity of being sinful, can obscure for us. It is so obvious and yet we so rarely glimpse it. But those brief glimpses are like sparks of light in the dark. They guide us, but we must have the courage to follow them. We have to have the courage to trust the light and to follow it even though darkness is all around us. That too we learn from our meditation. It sounds very easy but we soon know that it is not. It is the most demanding task that we have to fulfil. It isn't merely an option. It is a direct challenge, but it is the challenge of love. It is the challenge of being loved and of accepting that love, of knowing God and being known by him. It is that challenge which constitutes our meaning and our integrity, and so if we evade it we enter into meaninglessness and lose our integrity.

It often seems to people at the beginning of the path of meditation that the challenge is too great. It seems beyond our capacity to transcend ourselves and, of course, that is an absolutely essential insight to come to. Without it we remain in the illusion that we create and so redeem ourselves. We are in the state of primal pride, original sin. We have to understand and accept our limitations and insufficiency if we are really to be converted into Christians. Humility makes us all the more ready to be grateful for the gift of being and for every moment of life. It is given to us to respond to those gifts. Whatever the length of our life, that is all the time we are given to respond, and life is therefore urgent. The one word that would describe perhaps all the Gospels is 'urgency'; there is no time to waste. The Gospels tell us that if we don't respond now to the invitation to become fully alive our capacity remains limited. If we can respond, our capacity is potentially unlimited. It is simply a question of whether we believe that or not. Probably the worst condition to be in is half-belief. The difference can also be expressed as the difference between life experienced as limitation or as disappointment and life experienced, in the words of St John, as *eternal life*. And he has told us that *eternal life* does not mean 'life after death'. Eternal life – that quality of life which is boundless – is to know Jesus Christ and the One who sent him. That is the purpose of our meditation; to know this person. Meditation is the way into full life, because in that poverty of spirit we do come to know Jesus by following his commands. We come to know him as we come to know any one, by paying attention and by taking our thoughts off ourselves, by letting the other be and letting our own problems fall to one side.

To know someone is to have their spirit enter you, and therefore to 'know Jesus' is to be filled with his life, a life which takes us beyond ourselves, beyond sadness to joy. It takes courage to know anyone. It takes courage to know Jesus. It is the courage to let go of the half-life of our egoism. Courage is no less required to accept the gift of joy, because to accept any gift is to be placed into relationship by that acceptance. The saints are recognizable by their joy, by their laughter and their capacity to make others see and feel the joyfulness of life. That is the supreme power of Jesus. But it is a power that we have to have the courage (which only means the simplicity) to accept. It is a kind of heroic courage, but it is the heroism not of asserting ourselves but of self-affirming; and we have good reason to be joyful, good reason to allow Jesus to lead us from sadness to celebration. To have Jesus as our Teacher, to have heard his Word and to have felt his Word resonate in our hearts, leads to a supreme joy and an unshakeable confidence.

We have just celebrated the feast of Christ the King. Perhaps to understand why he is King we have to think of the symbol of kingship not in terms of modern monarchy or the exercise of power and domination but imaginatively to go back to the dawn of human history when people sought a king, a leader. They needed protection against enemies, against the anonymity of nature, to consolidate human fellowship. The leader-king was one who overcame the enemies. Jesus is the King of kings because he has overcome the supreme enemy of mankind, the enemy that no one else could defeat – the enemy that we are so frightened of that we don't even think about it, the enemy of death. In overcoming death he has carved out the way to a new kind of life. Death is what we succumb to when we choose existence rather than life. And, because of Christ, there is no reaon to make that choice. Our freedom is a burden until we accept the gift of it. The gift is freely offered, but we freely choose to accept it. The mantra is that choice. Every time we say it, we choose and we choose with our whole being in the depth of our spirit. We choose to be alive and to be alive in the life of Christ.

These words are from the Gospel of John. 'Simon Peter answered, "Lord, to whom shall we go? Your words are words of eternal life. We have faith and we know that you are the Holy One of God." ' That faith-knowledge is the starting-point of Christian meditation.

Holiness and Others

I suppose if we wanted to sum up John Main's teaching in terms of the tradition that he was passing on, one couldn't do better than read this sentence from *Word into Silence*. 'Cassian recommended anyone who wanted to learn to pray and to pray continually, to take a single short verse, to repeat this verse over and over again.' Every word there is well chosen. He recommended it to *anyone* who wanted to learn to pray. It is a tradition that is open to everyone. At the end of his Tenth Conference Cassian emphasizes that no one is excluded from this 'highest form of prayer'. But it is highest in no elitist way. It is the highest form because every follower of Christ has been called in their discipleship to the full development of their spirit. When he says that no one is excluded from this even by reason of lack of intelligence or lack of education he is saying what the Gospel stories often put before us – that it is the simple rather than the learned, the straightforward rather than the self-conscious, who find it easiest to learn to pray.

And he says there too that we are to pray *continually*. That is just what St Paul says, and he has the same way of expressing the call to Christian perfection as a universal call, in terms of continual prayer. Then there are the words, 'who want to learn to pray . . .' That is an important one for us to understand. We *want* to learn. We probably *want* to learn to do that more than anything else because we realize that everything else depends upon the fact that our spiritual potential is being realized. In other words, unless we are 'on the way' everything we do is hollow, two-dimensional.

If we are on the way then life has the dimension of Christ.

So we want to learn to pray. There is a natural longing for holiness in each of us, and we have to understand correctly what kind of longing and what kind of holiness is involved. It is important to understand because it has often been so abused and trivialized in the course of the Christian centuries. Often the desire for holiness has become so egotistical that it has run absolutely counter to the Gospel teaching of love, tolerance and compassion.

We have to understand that sanctification takes place within the community of disciples. There is no individualized holiness. Every enlightenment of every individual soul touches every other soul because it is the expansion of the enlightenment of Christ who is present in each – the building up of his enlightened Body, the perfection of his Church. So our longing for holiness originates from within our fellowship. And that is why we must face and answer that longing with practical communal steps, because our fellowship as disciples makes no sense without prayer. Holiness demands that we pray together. The Church becomes just a social, political or intellectual organization if we are not at prayer and deeply in prayer. And if we are not in prayer neither are we a witness, or at best we are a very unconvincing witness. That longing for holiness we experience within the Church, and which the Church itself sensitizes us to, is a perception of our being invited to holiness personally but as persons in community.

It also involves a sense of sin because we know that we are *not* whole, we have been divided by fear, by egoism, by individual and inherited mistakes. And yet we know too that in Christ we have been healed, made whole. And so our longing for holiness is always tempered, moderated, humbled by our awareness that we approach that holiness with absolutely no *rights*. It comes as complete gift and the Church, that fellowship of the teaching of Christ which is alive with his Spirit, helps us to find the balance between the sense of sin and the call to holiness. The call to holiness comes to us in the Body of Christ and it is in and through the Body that we are enabled to respond to that call. We would all like to settle for less because responding to that call is very demanding. It is an absolute call. We would like to say, 'Well, some are called to holiness but I am not. I am called to a reasonably good life. I'll settle down somewhere along the way.' But that is to deny Jesus who has called each and every one to fullness of life according to his or her own unique capacity. What that capacity is none of us know. All that is important is that we must be filled.

The call of Jesus is absolute and universal and that is what makes it impossible for us to settle for less. He told us that we must be holy as our heavenly Father is holy. And in those words he gives us the key to our vocation: 'as he is holy'. The Father is holy in himself. In himself, not as a result of any outside effect or effort. And so to be holy like him we have to enter into his self, into his holiness. Any desire for holiness outside of his holiness is illusion and egoism. In fact, when we can see it in this light we understand that the *desire* for holiness, in the ordinary possessive sense of that phrase, is itself an impediment to holiness. So how do we respond to the call? We respond by attentiveness, by simply turning away from our own selves which are for each of us a mixture of holiness and unholiness. We turn away from ourselves to the perfect holiness of God. What good does that do us? His holiness is in itself so utterly transcendent. How could we share in it? We can share in it through Jesus because the holiness of the Father lives in the Son and the Son lives in us. And so the holiness of the Father is immanent in us through the Spirit. And our own response to the vocation to be holy is our response to Jesus, to be attentive to him, to see him everywhere and in everyone. Not only in ourselves, perhaps least of all in ourselves, at first, but in others around us. And when we see him we shall be like him, for we shall see him as he is. That is what continual prayer means. 'Pray without ceasing,' says St Paul with all the masters of the teaching who have passed on the tradition. It means to enter into the continual prayer of Jesus which is his Spirit, which is complete attentiveness to the Father, and a going beyond himself to the Father's perfect holiness. We pray continually only because he prays continually with his undis-

tracted consciousness in us. The mantra simply leads us to be
deeply and permanently attentive to his prayer, to his Spirit
flowing in our hearts, flowing between him and the Father.

Every Christian community united in prayer works towards
the holiness of each and the holiness of the Body, together. It
is not a race where anyone is trying to get to the end first
because no one, in a sense, gets to the end before we all get
there and yet we have all got there because Jesus has got there
first. Any community rooted in prayer, turned towards Christ
as its living centre, aids each of us in mindfulness, attentiveness
to that spirit of continual prayer in the heart of each. To be
attentive to that is to see it. And to see it is to become it.

Letting Go

It is said that Gandhi was once approached by a woman who asked him to talk to her daughter who had become greatly addicted to sweets. She wanted Gandhi to give her the wisdom necessary to break her addiction. He told her to bring her daughter back to him in three weeks. So the woman went away and three weeks later she brought her daughter back to him and she listened as Gandhi spoke to her. He said it was very important for her not to be greedy, not to make a pig of herself by constantly eating sweets and cakes. He told her this gluttony was harmful to her body and her spirit. Then he told her to go now and not to overeat. And the girl went away. When the woman came up to Gandhi to thank him she asked him why he did not say that three weeks ago, and he replied that three weeks ago he himself was addicted to sweets.

We all begin the journey of meditation enchained, addicted to different things – to sweets, to self-indulgence, to fantasy, to the past. And we all begin the path of meditation at different points. The path of meditation leads us out of all slavery, all enchainment. It is a way of liberty. Yet the wonder of it is that it is the same journey for all of us at whatever stage we may be. It is only necessary to begin exactly where we are and to follow the road that stretches before us. As we do so we encounter a completely new experience in our life, an experience of communion with everyone else on the path and a growing sense of union with the whole of creation. Yet we all do begin with a certain egoism, and it is important to understand that meditation is not meant for the perfect but for human beings who know that they are called to be perfect; Jesus tells his disciples, 'Be perfect as your heavenly Father is perfect'. One of the problems we face as we begin to meditate, wherever we begin from, is the contrast between our present state of egoism and imperfection, and that apparently unattainable state of perfection. It is important to understand how to approach that contrast so that we can follow the path as we are meant to follow it.

One of the great dangers for religious or spiritual people is religious or spiritual egoism. Our very awareness of imperfection, egoism or sinfulness is an inevitable part of the spiritual and religious response to life. It is merely knowing that we are incomplete. We can be aware of that and humbly desire to be perfect and to leave egoism behind, but the desire for perfection can itself become a form of egoism. We can desire to possess perfection, to get ourselves enlightened and to possess holiness. That is why it is important to understand what our basic attitude should be as we follow the way of meditation. The tradition calls this attitude *apatheia*, desirelessness, non-possessiveness. The great power of meditation is to cut out the root of all egoism in us. This happens simply by turning our attention completely away from self, even from this self-conscious antithesis between present imperfection and the hoped-for future perfection. It takes our attention off that difference during our meditation and increasingly at all other times as well. As long as we are concentrating on that contrast we are thinking about ourselves, we are trapped in egoism. And one of the tricks of the ego is to convince us that we can leave egoism behind by becoming egotistical in another sort of way. But the way of meditation undercuts all the tricks of the ego because it is absolutely simple. The power of meditation in cutting out the root of egoism in us consists in taking our attention completely off ourselves.

That is the essential dynamic of the mantra. While we are saying the mantra we *cannot* be thinking of ourselves. We think neither of our egoism nor of our sanctity. We are turned away from self. That is why it is always so important at every step of the journey, and especially at the beginning, to understand that the *practice* of meditation is much more important than the *theory*. If you try to develop a complete theory of meditation it will take more than one lifetime and you would never get down to the practice of it. But the practice is utterly simple. It is important to meditate twice a day, every day. Most of us have a lot of ground to make up on the journey and so dedication of time and fidelity to the journey is absolutely necessary. During those times of meditation we must become absolutely simple and hence we restrict ourselves to the simplicity of the mantra. We sit down and we sit with stillness of body. The only basic rule of posture is to keep your back straight. Sit in a relaxed but reverent and alert way. Find a position you will be comfortable in but not too comfortable. Then lightly close your eyes, let the muscles of your face relax and begin to say your mantra. The mantra we recommend means 'Come Lord' and is the Aramaic word 'Maranatha'. Say it interiorly, silently, in the depths of your spirit, and as you say it, give it your full attention. Say the mantra with simplicity and fidelity from the beginning of the meditation right through to the end.

Learning to do any of those things – meditating every day, twice a day, learning to sit still, learning to say the mantra – all of those aspects of the way of meditation take time to learn. But that is all we have to learn. There are no advanced courses. If we can learn to do those things then we are launched on the way.

Sometimes we can accept the teaching at first with great enthusiasm. Then later, when we begin to feel the discipline involved, we can begin to question it. And it seems puzzling to us. If this is the path to perfection, shouldn't it be more sophisticated, more complex? Shouldn't we be doing something a little bit more advanced at this point, coming to grips with our imperfections more specifically? But gradually the experience itself begins to teach us. It teaches us through its own simplicity and through our fidelity that the way to go beyond egoism is simply to persevere humbly, but strongly, in taking the searchlight of consciousness off ourselves. Now that is easier said than done. But it can be done and it is done by saying the mantra.

If you say the mantra you have to face the consequences of saying the mantra and that will be the transformation of your life. As this conversion unfolds in our ordinary life, we begin to recognize it as the redemptive experience, the experience of liberation. Although we may think of ourselves at the beginning as chained to many things, we are in fact only chained to ourselves. The liberty we long for is precisely the liberty from self-consciousness, self-centredness, self-obsession, from isolation. We long for the liberty and the joy of that liberty. It is the freedom to pass beyond ourselves and our limitations into the unlimited mystery of God's perfect love. As we do so, we fulfil the purpose of our creation, to become who we are called to be. So in saying the mantra don't be concerned with your imperfections or your hopes for perfection. Your only concern is to discover who you are. We don't know yet who we are but we come to know that we are a person created by love for love.

In the Christian vision the power of this liberation flows into us from the liberated, resurrected life of Jesus. The perfection, the enlightenment that we discover is not our own but his, his light which enlightens everyone who comes into the world, and his perfection which he shares with us. Because we are centred in him, we need not be concerned about ourselves and the way can therefore be a way of complete simplicity, complete unselfconsciousness. But it is a way of faith. There is work involved in being faithful but it is a simple work. It is the work of the mantra to lead us faithfully on the journey.

This is the experience of liberation that St Paul wrote about to the Romans:

It follows, my friends, that our lower nature has no claim upon us; we are not obliged to live on that level. . . . For all who are moved by the Spirit of God are sons of God. The spirit you have received is not a spirit of slavery leading you back into a life of fear, but a Spirit that makes us sons, enabling us to cry 'Abba, Father!' In that cry the Spirit of God joins with our spirit in testifying that we are God's children. (Rom. 8:12, 14–16)

Time is Sacred

There is a sentence in Father John's teaching on the mantra which gives a valuable insight into the journey we are making. It is a very simple sentence. 'If you chop and change your mantra you are postponing your progress in meditation.' It is an interesting statement from him because he wouldn't talk about how long it would take to achieve the end of meditation. But he did recognize the fact that we could make progress and therefore that we could postpone progress. The tradition of the teaching we follow is there to encourage us. It isn't there just to give us new ideas or to make us better writers or talkers on meditation. It is there to bring us back, time and time again, to the one essential task we have. The teaching is there to strengthen us because, being human, we need to be strengthened and we need to be strengthened with the same food. Our hope is strengthened, our faith is strengthened and if we meet with failure then we need to be encouraged, strengthened and inspired to start again. We should even come to see our failure in a completely unegotistical light – not to see it merely as a failure to succeed but to understand that it is a failure to respond to love. If we can see it in that way then failure, in fact, becomes a means to touch an even greater depth.

It is when we look at the love that is there in the depth, rather than at ourselves, that we are led into self-knowledge. So the teaching is there for depth, to encourage. It is not there to lead to complacency. It isn't that failure is all right: we should fail less and less. The teaching is constantly educating us out of complacency, but part of our complacency is to accept failure too readily and that is what we call compromise. There is a sharp little point of pure idealism in the journey we are making – the sharp little point of the Absolute, and it won't go away. It is the standard by which we mark the route.

Out of that sharp little point the teaching comes to us, uncompromising, but human, loving, Christlike. The teaching therefore takes us out of our tendency to compromise and be complacent. Yet it doesn't make us anxious. Being shaken out of our complacency in other areas of life – in a marriage, a career, in our health – tends to make us nervous and anxious about failure and success, but to be shaken out of complacency on the spiritual path (which is the *whole* path of life) means, in fact, that we are brought into a deeper peace. But it is an experience that we can have only if we allow ourselves to be shaken. It is a sobering and even shocking thought that we *can* waste time. We are too easy on ourselves sometimes by thinking that everything happens as it should. No doubt it does in one way. But that isn't to say that, if we allow ourselves to be touched by that pure point or absolute teaching, things couldn't turn out a different way. We can postpone our progress. In fact, as we all know, we all do.

The reason that that need not lead us to despair is because of the teaching presence of Christ and the influence of his redemptive love. But wasting time demands a price from us. It demands that we make up the time that we lose. The nature of the journey, the demand of our destiny, is that we have to make up lost time. Making up for lost time causes most of what we think of as the difficulties of the journey. The journey should be a great deal smoother. It wouldn't ever be without difficulties, without 'persecutions'. But it could be a great deal more joyful and more of a witness to the world.

What is our progress and how can we waste time? Our progress is the penetrating of the present moment, living life with our feet on the ground, living in compassionate, active relationship with others, and yet living in the awareness that life has been penetrated by the eternal moment of God and unfolds in the power of that moment. Our anxious thoughts for yesterday or for tomorrow are, in fact, blocking the power of that eternal moment because they are confronting illusion against reality.

And so we repeatedly ask ourselves how can we live in the present moment? The answer is very simple. It is not to waste time. That means something very practical in the daily life of everyone of us. Not to waste time in trivia, not to waste time in distraction, and certainly not to seek distraction. Not to plan our time to include sections when we allow ourselves distraction. That is sheer waste of time. It isn't so much the things we do as the reasons we do them. The distraction is in the motive not in the deed. We can be wasting time equally in busyness or in idleness.

Every Christian fellowship committed to the present moment will be aware of the value of time, indeed the sacredness of time as well as of the sacrilegious stupidity of wasting it. Such a community is a community that is open to the power of God that can only be experienced in his own present moment, not in our time-centred imagining. In such a community and for all those whom that community can touch, loneliness becomes solitude, and solitude becomes the basis of communion. Sadness is dispelled by the directing of our efforts to another's happiness. That is the dynamic of meditation, of staying with the mantra, with the same mantra. That is the dynamic of our meditation in our ordinary life and why it transforms our ordinary life into the life of God.

Love that Divinizes

He came and proclaimed the good news: peace to you who were far off and peace to those who were nearby; for through him we both alike have access to the Father in the one Spirit. (Eph. 2:17–18)

The path of meditation is a process of coming to know the meaning of these words in an utterly personal way, to know that they are not simply the expression of a theological truth but of a personal reality. At the simplest and most basic level the way meditation does that is by making us aware of the meaning of one of those words we use most frequently and perhaps understand least – the word 'spirit'.

In Father John's vision the first purpose of the silence of meditation is to allow us to find our own spirit. That is why meditation is a journey of discovery, an uncovering of something that we are not familiar with. It is a journey into the unknown, a journey into the discovery that we are known. As we become more silent we become more conscious of what the spirit is, because we awaken more consciously in the spiritual dimension of our being. We come to realize that the spirit is a different dimension from either mind or body and also that the spirit is not so much *in* the body, like a ghost in a machine, nor just in the mind – but is much more a mysterious point although it is beyond space, in which mental and bodily processes are united and transcended.

I suppose when we speak like this it sounds esoteric, intellectual or very abstract. But it is only a way of expressing the utterly real and rooted experience of meditation which is the process of integration and of coming to know who we are. We then come to be able to read the words of the New Testament, for example the word 'Spirit', from a personal basis of experience of what it means to be spiritual and spiritually alive. We come to see, as St Paul taught, that the spiritual is the immortal part of us, the infinite point which absorbs the mortal and the finite. It is in the spirit that mind and body are united. This discovery of our own spirit is the work of integration and of the harmonization that we increasingly feel meditation is accomplishing. It is often disturbing because, as we feel it being accomplished, it also becomes more difficult to define. We feel more confident about our definitions before it begins to take place. As it takes place we realize, in the reality of the experience, just how inadequate our words, all words are. The experience slips out of the mind's attempt to possess it. We ask, 'What is the spirit?' and we find it less and less easy to answer. It would be easier to answer if one could make a clear opposition between those different aspects of our being which are the aspects we encounter in our daily life, our relationships and in our reflection on the mystery of life, the dimensions of body, mind and spirit.

But as we make the journey of meditation we come to realize that we cannot make final oppositions between those three dimensions, because in discovering our spirit we also become more rooted, more real, in those other dimensions too. This is the way that we come to simplicity, although it *seems* perhaps a complex route when we analyse it. But it brings us to the purifying simplicity of being unable to answer our own basic questions. This is the encounter with mystery, and we are then challenged either to become simple or to go back into complexity. But there is really no turning back. To ask, 'What is the spirit?' is really asking 'Who am I?' That is as simple a question as there is. And it is a question that can only be answered by knowing, 'I am the person who is asking the question.' When we encounter that level of powerful and purifying simplicity, the simplicity of pure being which we discover at the level of spirit, we also travel deeper into silence.

Silence is where the final question has been left behind, where we are no longer trying to find answers but where we are beginning to open ourselves to the reality beyond question and answer.

At the point where we leave questions behind, where we ask unanswerable questions, like the *koan*, we also discover a kind of absurdity, a kind of foolishness. It is the absurdity of the ego trying to master the spirit. It is the absurdity of trying to probe the mystery of spirit with the tools of the mind. I suppose an even more tragic kind of absurdity is the result of trying to grasp the spirit through the body as one might try through drugs. Our only response in the face of simplicity of that unanswerable kind is humility, and that is why the simplicity of our meditation gradually smashes our ego . . . if we will remain simple for long enough. To remain simple is to journey in the spirit. The spirit is the utterly simple and basic identity of who we are, the irreducible person we are, the person God knows and loves. The spirit enfolds mind and body and every dimension of our life, bringing all its dimensions to fulfilment and their full potential, *when* we can allow the spirit free play. And that is the work of our meditation, learning to be. This is the work of the silence of our meditation in which we let our consciousness travel naturally to its own starting point, which is the centre of our being where we come forth from God, the point where we are at one with ourselves and with the Spirit of God. And if all this sounds just an interior journey then we are only hearing part of the story, because to be spiritual is to be loving. To be spiritual and unloving is a contradiction in terms.

At this level of spirit we experience the love that creates us, the love that redeems us and the love that sanctifies us. The love of God: Father, Son and Spirit. As we become more spiritual we become more loving and we learn that God is love, discovering this in every encounter of the day and every relationship, because these three divine dimensions of love – creative, redemptive and sanctifying – are perceptible in every human experience of love. The discipline of loving each other makes us more spiritual. One love leads to the other. The commandment 'to love one another' is the essence of Jesus' spiritual teaching to his disciples because all love creates, redeems and sanctifies. All love divinizes and all love elicits true identity, the true identity that each of us is an ikon of God, created and loved in his image and likeness. As we know, following the journey from day to day, we often fear to become spiritual because we fear losing the other dimensions of our being or, to put it another way from another level of experience, we fear to love because we fear losing ourselves. Meditation overcomes the fear which denies life and restricts expansion into fullness of life. It frees us from fear simply by letting us find our own spirit. In finding it we uncover the love of God creative, redemptive and sanctifying flowing in us through the Spirit of Christ.

So he came and proclaimed the good news: peace to you who were far off and peace to those who were nearby; for through him we both alike have access to the Father in the one Spirit. . . . In him the whole building is bonded together and grows into a holy temple in the Lord. In him you too are being built with all the rest into a spiritual dwelling for God. (Eph. 2:17–18, 21–2)

Harmonious Unity

Plato said that philosophy begins with wonder. I think the religious response to life might well be seen as an exploring of that wonder, not only of thinking, philosophizing or talking about it. The religious response is a way of entering the mystery which is the very cause of wonder and knowing that we will be transformed by entering it. Although it is a mystery beyond our powers of understanding, we are invited to *know* it, indeed to love and serve it. We are invited to explore that mystery and the wonderful exploration is what we call 'our spiritual path'. This is the path of meditation.

Of the great symbols used in all traditions to describe this exploration, many describe it as a journey, an adventure, a pilgrimage. We are involved in a kinetic experience if we make our response and if we remain on the path. We are not simply looking at the mystery. We are advancing into it. And that is why we grow on the daily path of meditation. There is inevitable change, development. Science is to us the most obvious way of exploring the world's mystery of creation because it takes us into the visible world outside of us. But we are finding today – as I suppose the first scientists also found – that science leads right back to the sublimely simple questions of the spiritual path and to the primal sense of wonder. Wonder is a quality of childlike consciousness. Children wonder at very simple things, the evident and mundane things: What is spirit? What is mind? Where did matter come from? What is energy? What is life? Those very basic questions are the source of our wonder, but they are only the beginning of the spiritual path.

The spiritual path does not run counter to the other questionings and explorings of our life. Any truly spiritual path, like meditation, does indeed take us within to an interior universe. But it also leads beyond ourselves into a consciousness deeper than self-consciousness and into a way of being and perception in which we are taken beyond ourselves. This is what is called 'liberty' in the New Testament, liberty of spirit. We are led into the wonder of creation at each of its levels, and the great wonder is that we are empowered to allow our lives to blend with the lives of others, to enter into relationship, to love. The real test of progress on the path of meditation is not growth in abstract conceptual knowledge, which depends on the kind of mind one has, but growth in charity, which is the capacity to love. This is why the one essential command that Jesus gave is to love one another. Jesus, the supreme Master and Teacher of love tells us that love will lead us to all Wisdom. But we need (and in our own society we need this more urgently than ever before) an interior path, a way to come into a full knowledge of ourselves before we *can* relate to the world and to people around us at sufficient depth to love.

Meditation is a simple path. It is as simple as walking. You put one foot in front of another and you take one step at a time. It is as simple as walking but it is as demanding as a pilgrimage, because it asks us to *continue* walking so that we don't turn back and that we don't sit down and wait for the destination to come to us. Meditation, being a spiritual path, shows us that reality, which is the source as well as the goal of the journey, is not an opposition of inner and outer, of matter and spirit. The path shows us that reality is one and that anything real is unified. Such is the fundamental revelation of the Bible, that God is One. Consequently, it is the fundamental revelation of the New Testament that all creation is restored to unity with the One who is God by Christ. Meditation is the spiritual path that brings us to the fully personal experience of the oneness of reality, to the one God. It brings us into a unifying personal experience of that Truth, not into any second-hand report about it. We are not experiencing what we have *read*. We are not experiencing what somebody else has described to us. The wisdom and teaching of others, the tradition, is vital to guide and keep us on course. Nor can we make the journey alone. But the experience to which it calls us is a fully personal and self-authenticating one.

First of all, meditation integrates *us*. It leads us to a unity: a unity of mind and heart, a unity of body and spirit. All the different elements of ourselves that we so often think compete with each other or oppose each other meet at one point, a centrepoint of personal consciousness where we see all these different dimensions to be 'one'. As we come to experience ourselves as a unity our inner and outer lives are brought into harmony.

Unity and harmony. These are both terms used to describe the experience of reality, which Jesus called the 'Kingdom'. Meditation itself is a unified and harmonious path to find this Kingdom within us and then to know from that realm of interiority that we are within the Kingdom as well. It is a path of unity typified by taking one word with us on this journey and leaving behind all other words, concepts, imagery, and philosophy. We embrace one single 'poor' word, and restrict ourselves to the sounding of it in our heart during the periods of meditation. All language and thought are, as it were, concentrated into the simplicity of this single word or phrase which unifies all the expressive parts of our being. This word that we call a mantra is a sacred word repeated continuously from the beginning to the end of each meditation. To make the journey real we have to set aside real time to make it. We set aside about thirty minutes each morning and each evening. During that time we leave to one side all thoughts, problems, plans, analysis of the past, and anxiety about the future. Eventually we leave ourself behind – which is what Jesus has called us to do: in order to follow him all the way on his journey we must leave ourself behind.

A dimension of the unity we come to experience is unity with the body. In order to achieve the experience of that unity we have to learn the discipline of physical stillness, just as we have to learn through the saying of the mantra the discipline of interior, mental stillness. Lightly close your eyes. Sit with your back straight. Sit relaxed but alert. Then silently, interiorly, begin to say and continue to say, in faith and love, your single word, the word leading to unity. The mantra is not something to think about but to say. So don't think about its meaning; listen to it. It is above all in *listening* to it as we say it that we are unified. *Listening* explains the mantra as a way to harmony because we listen to it just as we listen to a harmonic – a sound which is sounded within us, not nonsensical, not without meaning but containing and expressing all meaning and so unifying all expressions of meaning. This harmonic sets up a resonance within us, like a tuning fork. The resonance is our harmony with Christ, with his life, his life-rhythm and his life-energy in us, and Christ resonates in harmony with God. That is why to be in Christ is to be in God. This is why Jesus said that he is the Way to the Father.

This is a way of describing meditation in the Christian vision, but at the times of meditation, morning and evening, we are probably more aware of the psychological difficulty of saying the mantra and that it requires a discipline, a continual return to it, not allowing our unavoidable distractions to prevent us from saying it. We are also aware, especially in the first few months, that there is a discipline in learning to meditate twice a day, every day and staying on the path, coming back to it whenever we have dropped it. But this Christian sense of meaning in the discipline and its ascesis does, without fail, really emerge. First comes the experience of faith, and then the meaning of the experience emerges and becomes our own personal meaning, something that gives meaning to *this* life. There is always the temptation to leave the path, to go off looking for or following distractions, to be dissatisfied with our 'progress', restless, impatient or just discontented. The mantra will recall us from that temptation. It leads to silence, to a silence we discover to be not of negation, but of resonance. The silence is our resonance with Christ and his resonance with the Father. That is the vision in which we follow the very simple and humble path of meditation. It is a marvellous and authentic vision of reality and one that we are all called to see for ourselves. It is a vision that requires commitment and discipline, and it takes us time to learn that discipline and commitment. But it is as simple as sitting down and saying the mantra.

To prepare for meditation consider the vision of the unity of all creation in Christ that St Paul describes in the Letter to the Ephesians:

He has made known to us his hidden purpose – such was his will and pleasure determined beforehand in Christ – to be put into effect when the time was ripe: namely, that the universe, all in heaven and on earth, might be brought into a unity in Christ. (Eph. 1:9–10)

Meeting the Other

At some point along the journey we begin to understand that meditation is teaching us the most important of all lessons: how to love and be loved. It also teaches us the living truth of Jesus' teaching, that we have to die and leave self behind. That is exactly the same teaching as 'Love your neighbour'. To love is to let somebody *be*. This means to be prepared to give their being priority, to give them your being and in that readiness, which is total attentiveness to the other, we experience the loss of our own self.

We learn this lesson not intellectually but within the incarnate reality of our life. Yet I think we also have to understand how learning this truth is part of the experience of the whole human family and how learning it establishes a bond between us and the world we live in. No one living in our society can be unaware that we live among tensions which have become so great in recent history that they have polarized into extreme and violently opposed forces. Yet one of the beatitudes of being a Christian is that we are blessed, meaning happy, because we make peace. I think meditation leads us to understand that paradox of being a peacemaker in a violent world, not in vague generalities but specifically. It helps us to understand how our commitment to meditation is commitment to Christ present in the world and how it is therefore a practical commitment to the peace and love of his spirit. Our way of meditation is in a most real sense a way of peace linked spiritually and psychologically to the world of tensions, violence and distrust that we are all part of and, in part, responsible for. We learn fairly soon after we begin to meditate that we do not meditate for our own selves or for our own private peacefulness alone.

Because in the poverty of the mantra we have begun to leave self behind, we discover that meditation generates innumerable ways of contributing to the strengthening of peace in the world through selfless relationships and responsibilities. We learn that the degree to which we have left self behind is the degree to which the peace of Christ is made available to the world through us. Whatever benefits may accrue to us through our meditation are not there merely for us to possess. They become the common benefit of all, because there is less and less of an ego to possess the peace, joy and liberty that meditation brings. Yet even though the fruits of the Spirit are a general inheritance the tradition has always emphasized the necessity of finding them ourselves by coming to full self-knowledge. It emphasizes this as a first step in becoming a disciple of Jesus, because when we have found our true self we have found freedom to make the energy of our discovery, all its peace and joy, part of the common fund, the common experience of the human family. When we have begun to know our true self that self-knowledge, which is our spirit, becomes a fully contributing part of the human family and, as in all true families, everything is shared. Whatever is ours belongs to others. The wonder and mystery of growing up in such a spiritual family is that we experience, in the most practical and down-to-earth way, our spiritual path, our prayer, as the builder of community and maker of peace.

In order to realize this we must learn that we have a demanding journey to make. It is the most demanding of all journeys but it is the only journey. We know that we have to leave self behind and that we cannot leave self behind until we have found and entered our own solitude. We cannot begin to understand our incorporation in the human family until we have begun to understand and experience our solitude. We must understand clearly what that means. We can meditate alone but we can *never* meditate in isolation. We cannot find ourself or come to self-knowledge in isolation. If we try to, we will only persist in re-finding the ego. It is only in the experience of otherness, of being turned towards the other and in awakening to the other, that we can become ourself. We fear otherness because we fear that the little degree of reality we have worked to gain will be lost if we come close to the reality of another. There is a certain logic in that fear, but there is no reason to be held back from doing it by that fear. Truth lies behind every fear. To find it we must unmask the fear.

The truth is that we cannot be left unchanged by encountering another. That is the truth expressed unforgettably in that haunting phrase, 'no one can see God and live'. God is *the* Other, the reality of Reality. He is our real-ness. The depth of our own encounter with another is the degree to which we are changed. We are changed, however, into our real self. The deepest encounter is the greatest change and that is undergone in death. But Jesus has taught us and is with us to remind us that we can approach the Other even in death without fear. Indeed in the light of his consciousness we can even understand that our whole life is simply a progressive encounter with the Other who is God. Every relationship of our life, every turning towards another, is an ever-deepening encounter with the Other in whose image we are made. When we allow ourselves to experience this, which we do when we meditate and when we love, we discover that our fear can only finally be dispelled by the encounter itself and that the deeper the encounter each time, the less fear survives it. It can seem that it should be the other way around – that we will fear the Other the more we encounter it – but because the reality of otherness is love it casts out fear more completely the more perfect it becomes.

There need be no fear because otherness does not mean the state of opposition, tension or hostility. The other, when we have turned towards it, is not opposite. The experience of otherness does not polarize but unites. It reveals not increasing difference but deepening similarity, correspondence not dissonance.

Until we have had the courage to face and encounter the other we have not yet found ourself. Until then we are always other to ourself. We are a stranger to ourself. That is the state of egoism, being an alien to our own self. In that state all others are opposite to us, opposed to us. We experience, both individually and socially, a state of fear rather than love, a state of rejection rather than hospitality. We experience sadness, mistrust and violence. The first step out of this hell is to have the courage to encounter ourself as ourself, no longer as other, or as a stranger to ourself. By our own inner resources none of us could do that. We would be forever unredeemed if it were not for the intervening love of God. The destiny that has led us to meditate and to know the relationships of love that are the incarnation of our encounter with God is the sign in our lives of his redemptive love.

When we meditate we learn to leave all images of ourself behind because the images are strangers to our real self. They are like inaccurate labels. Our labelling self-analysis, which we think to be so clever, isolates us from the knowledge of the real self and from the redemptive encounter with reality. We imprison ourself in self-consciousness. We have only to understand that we have been liberated and that perfect liberty is achieved in the depth of our spirit in the liberty of Christ, the liberty of his pure love. We can turn to that reality if only we can learn to be simple, to accept the freely given gift and to be faithful to the gift. If we learn to say the mantra it teaches us how to love, and it will teach us how to expand beyond all images of ourself into the reality of ourself as one with the reality of Christ. It will teach us to be ourself and to know the joy of being in communion. This is the union with Christ described in the Letter to the Romans:

> If we have become incorporate with him in a death like his, we shall also be one with him in a resurrection like his. We know that the person we once were has been crucified with Christ, for the destruction of the sinful self, so that we may no longer be the slaves of sin . . . But if we thus died with Christ, we believe that we shall also come to life with him. We know that Christ, once raised from the dead, is never to die again. . . . For in dying as he died, he died to sin, once

for all, and in living as he lives, he lives to God. In the same way you must regard yourselves as dead to sin and alive to God, in union with Christ Jesus. (Rom. 6:5-6, 8-10)

Leaving Needs Behind

Just as we sometimes don't know our real capacity until we are challenged to go beyond what we think is our capacity, so the real depth of a teaching is sometimes only revealed when that teaching is challenged. Very often Father John's teaching was challenged by people who said, 'You are asking too much. The way of meditation is no doubt very good and you are a very remarkable person who can follow it but not everyone is remarkable, not everyone is as strong, as balanced, as integrated. Maybe you can do it. Maybe you can find a few people who can, but this is not a universal way. It is too poor, too rigorous, too demanding.' He would respond to that very strongly. He would feel disappointed because most often that challenge came from religious or priests, people who have a special responsibility for serving and ministering the gospel to all the people of God. He was disappointed that these people so under-estimated the gospel and the capacity of people to respond to the gospel–call.

He responded to their challenge simply by pointing to the Gospel. If this way of meditation is too demanding, he said, then the call of Jesus is too demanding. If it is unrealistic to expect the average person to meditate, it is unrealistic to expect the average person to be a follower of Christ because the way of meditation is essentially following the teaching of Jesus to leave self behind and to follow him. It isn't a call to follow a way of saintly perfection. It isn't a call to be a hero or a genius, nor even a call to be extraordinary in any way. It is a call to be the person you are and to take the time it takes to be who you are (whether it is five years or fifty years): the person whom Jesus has loved by laying down his life for him.

So Father John would point to the Gospel and would say that the teaching of meditation is the teaching of the Gospel. He says in *Word into Silence*, 'the whole of the teaching of Cassian on prayer is based on the Gospel,' and he quotes Jesus' words: 'In your prayers do not go babbling on like the heathen who imagine that the more they say, the more likely they are to be heard. Do not imitate them. Your Father knows what your needs are before you ask him.'

Those are indeed challenging and demanding words but they are addressed to everyone and no one can be themselves unless they respond to them with the seriousness and sincerity with which we are all called to respond.

Meditation is the context in which we respond. I think anyone who meditates can understand that it is not arrogant for us to say that it is *because* we are meditating that we can respond. What Jesus called on people to do was very simple. He would stop by somebody sitting at their work and he would look at them and say, 'Follow me'. That was all. And if they got up and followed him they were responding, they were now on the way. The significant point that the gospel makes is how important it was for them after this to stay with him. The gospel describes how, as he came closer to Jerusalem, many people found his teaching too hard and left him. Those who stayed with him were a rather unremarkable lot. They all eventually ran away for a moment – the moment of supreme testing – but by that time it didn't really matter. They had stayed with him and when they used to talk about progress or rewards, he would gently stop them. Time was short and the time given to them had to be used in following him, more fully, more unconditionally, more lovingly. That perseverance, in fact, was their progress.

There is a great demand in the words of Jesus 'that your Father knows what your needs are before you ask him'. It is the summons to be silent. It is the invitation to trust. Silence in meditation is the supreme expression of our trust in God, just as in any human relationship it can be the supreme expression of personal trust. From the experience of meditation we know that the demand at first evokes something frightening and almost impossible to understand: Leave your needs behind. And how can we leave our needs behind? Our need for personal fulfilment, our need for sympathy, our need for understanding, our need for recognition, our need for every essential kind of human affirmation. Leaving those needs behind seems to us to be almost impossibly negative until we understand that hanging on to them is the sure way of remaining *in need*. Hanging on to our needs is a denial of the fullness that we are offered in the present moment. When they are clung to, those needs are really not needs but desires.

How do we let go of them? Meditation tells us very simply. We let go of them by not asking for them, by not petitioning for them, at least not in an egotistical way. Not asking for *me*. Every prayer of the Mass is a petition but it is the need of the community in which each has transcended or is transcending his own isolated desires and egoism. When we pray for the coming of the Kingdom we are, as it were, throwing our own isolated needs and desires behind us and sacrificing ourself to the Kingdom, as a preparation for communion. Needs are also left behind by ceasing to think about them. That perhaps is the greatest challenge: to turn away even from thinking about our needs, in the trust that the Kingdom is established, and that its fullness is realized to the degree that we trust. If only we can trust.

It is easy to go around all day thinking about ourselves. We do it without being aware of it. Self-obsession becomes such a habit, like a mannerism we are unconscious of. We can go around turning over our needs, our deep needs or our immediate ones. We can go around thinking about how to cultivate our spiritual life, how to become perfect. How to become all the things we *want* or *need* to be, thinking about our progress, thinking about our comfort, physical or emotional. We shape today and tomorrow according to our needs and our wants. What I want to be. What I want to happen. Here is the hidden danger of the religious life, that it gives us so much time to think about nothing except ourselves and our needs. We have to face that danger within the life we live because if we do live it in self-absorption it would be no life at all but sheer illusion. We require the courage to shatter that ever-recurring illusion while it re-forms itself in us, to dismantle it by going back to our meditation with daily fidelity.

From the outside, the round of the monastic life can look very self-cultivating. But it isn't. It is directed God-wards and this is made very practical in directing ourself to others, to the service of the community, of each other and of those who come to us. A community which is always welcoming and open to others is simply a fellowship of those who are following Jesus on the Way, the way to Jerusalem, where he abandoned all personal needs, knowing that his Father knew them. To Jerusalem where, by the abandonment of Gethsemani, every need was fulfilled in the garden of the resurrection. The true monk is a type of Christian who is not thinking about his needs but is attending to God and his Kingdom, who is not thinking about his reward for following Christ, but is discovering with wonder and delight the great privilege of being able to follow him.

Rich Poverty

It would be impossible to meditate without coming to understand what poverty really is and what poverty of spirit involves. The knowledge that we are poor is one of the most healing and surprising experiences that meditation opens to us. It is also the sure confirmation that we are still on the journey; much more than spiritual success, the experience of poverty confirms that we are on course. In knowing poverty of spirit we know ourselves. We come progressively into a self-knowledge of a kind and of a depth that will always take us by surprise.

Reality is always surprising. It takes us unawares but the surprise then remains with us as a growing sense of wonder. At first the experience of poverty seems strange, unfamiliar, even hostile. We have to learn, by enduring in poverty, to recognize it for what it is and to see that this heart-felt experience, which reaches deep into our lives, is precisely what Jesus was talking about in the beatitudes. 'Blessed [happy] are the poor in spirit for theirs is the Kingdom of Heaven.' Recognizing that these words of Jesus apply to us constitutes the great transformation of our life. However we have first to learn to recognize poverty and then learn to remain poor. Living it, we can understand why Cassian, writing about meditation, called it a way of 'grand poverty'.

Poverty of spirit is an essential human experience to pass through. If we don't pass through it, we don't break into reality. And that means that we neither break into the reality of ourselves or discover the destiny that each of us has in God. We call it *poverty* only because material poverty is a metaphor for us to understand this spiritual condition. It is called poverty because poverty is a state where we have touched rock-bottom (the ground of our being), where we have no further resources of our own while remaining dependent on our Creator. Theoretically or theologically there is nothing very special about that. The lived experience of it, however, is cataclysmic. It is knowing who we are. It is being simply realistic. Poverty of spirit is almost another term for reality. When we are genuinely poor we can see ourselves, our life and relationships in a bright, clear light. However, we resist this poverty instinctively and a kind of gravitational force pulls us away from it because we prefer the illusion of ourselves as being independent of our Creator. In that false light of independent status we develop the Luciferian, egotistical notion of having a *relationship* with God as a relationship of equals. We lose the humble realism of understanding that because of his utter generosity we have *communion* with him, which is something much greater than relationship. We live and move and have our being in him. The illusion of independence costs us the reality of the freedom of being a child of God.

For as long as we resist the clear light of poverty our vision is blurred. It is rather like the difference in going to the top of Mount Royal, on which our monastery is built, in the middle of winter and looking out over the city and the St Laurence River, towards the mountains of Vermont. In the middle of winter you can see right to the hills on the horizon in the cold, clear light. In the middle of summer it is so hazy you can hardly see to the bottom of the mountain. Heavy heat-haze distorts and blurs everything. The clear vision that poverty gives us is one that stretches right to the border of our being, and yet reveals its true meaning only if we accept and stay long enough in it. The problem is that once we see the frontier of our being we want to run away from it. The perspective is too much and we resist it. No doubt this is due to, or at least is intensified for us today by, our social conditioning. A materialistic society teaches us to deny the reality of human limitations, to avoid poverty and see it as failure. Failure in our success-oriented society is an evil, something that always negates or diminishes life.

The Christian vision of poverty challenges that blurred view because its vision comes from Christ's perspective and has its focus set on the cross and the resurrection. With that focus we come to see failure quite differently. Not that we set out intentionally to be failures but we come to see the poverty of failure as part, one part but an essential part, of the mystery of life's unfolding, of its onward development and expansion. The resurrection shows us that the cross was once a failure and so reminds us that there is no full life that can claim to have no failures in it. It isn't enough for us to see this theologically and admit it on paper or in discussion. If it is going to have redemptive meaning we have to enter into it personally. Only in that personal participation will our vision be really clarified and extended.

The cross shows us that poverty of spirit is itself a kind of failure. But it teaches us not to resist failure because it reveals it as the failure of the human spirit to move beyond itself, its mortal frontiers, by its own resources. If we want to understand poverty of spirit we have to accept it as the reaching of the boundaries of our being and our capacity, and finding we are unable to go further by ourselves. Yet we know that we do go further. We know the cross stretches out into the limitless expanse of the resurrection. Beyond our frontier is the realm of God.

Poverty of spirit is a 'grand poverty' because when we have touched this boundary of being (that *is* the cross: *touching* it), it surprisingly recedes and marvellously our being expands. That is the resurrection. We don't necessarily recognize what the power of that expansion is. It takes time to recognize it as the personal power of Jesus, his being in which there are no boundaries, the new being of the resurrection, filling and stretching our limited consciousness.

We will not recognize that immediately. But every time we pass through a cross, every time we touch the boundary, our frontier is pushed forward. Each time his person is seen in a sharper and purer light. We do this every time we meditate. Prayer thus gives an ultimate meaning to our experience of poverty in every life situation. The mantra leads us to this boundary. It leads us there and holds us there until the time for expansion has come. It teaches us to wait because the gift of resurrection, of expansion, is in the Lord's giving.

The temptation is to shrink back from the boundary itself. That is felt as the temptation to stop saying the mantra, to resist the experience of poverty. Or, much the same thing, to try to make the failure a success by possessing the poverty. We do this usually by day-dreaming, by fantasy, by dreaming about success, in one form or another. We also do it by triviality, by postponement. It is our continuous fidelity to the mantra that takes us beyond triviality and day-dreaming, beyond the purgatory of endless postponement, to where we are destined to go. The cross is the great inspiration. Calvary teaches us not to evade but to embrace poverty and to breathe in an ever-deeper poverty so that we live from within the boundless riches of Christ. The secret of the Gospel has been proclaimed many times and yet ours, like every generation, must learn to rediscover it personally. It is the secret hidden for long ages, as St Paul says:

> . . . and through many generations, but now disclosed to God's people, to whom it was his will to make it known – to make known how rich and glorious it is among all nations. The secret is this: Christ in you, the hope of a glory to come. . . . and to come to the full wealth of conviction which understanding brings, and grasp God's secret. That secret is Christ himself; in him lie hidden all God's treasures of wisdom and knowledge. (Col. 1:26–7; 2:2–3)

Seeing God

It is one of the characteristics of being human that we need metaphors. It might be useful to reflect on the metaphor of vision that we use so often in relation to meditation. It helps to look at it in connection with the other great metaphor of the spiritual life, the journey. John Main described how he asked his teacher how long the journey of meditation would take and how his teacher simply looked away whenever he asked that question. Father John himself used to deal with that question, when others put it to him later, either by making them realize what a ridiculous question it was or by ignoring it. I suppose the best way to answer it is to ignore it and, if we can, we take a further step in faith towards meditating without analysing progress. This is something we feel we have to learn to do but something which it seems will take us a long time. The time is shortened when we realize that time itself is metaphorical.

How long will it take? underlies the other questions that slow us down on the journey: 'How fast am I going?' 'What progress am I making?' Projecting ourself into the future in this way simply has the result of alienating ourself from a direct experience of the present. When Father John refused to answer the question, he was in fact directly answering it by manifesting the present moment and doing so in the only way that it can be adequately communicated, which is in silence. How long? and how fast? – these are questions we may ask of all journeys except meditation, because they are questions of time and space. Meditation is a journey into God and the more we are absorbed in the reality of God the fainter become the dimensions of time and space and so the freer becomes our consciousness and liberty of spirit. We can apply the dimensions of time and space to the journey into God only as metaphors. They are important as metaphors but as soon as we forget they are metaphors we lose our focus. We are separate again, out of touch, and we fall back into the restricted orbit of our self-consciousness. When we face this question as we try to meditate day by day, it recapitulates the experience undergone by the early Church. They had begun to ask: 'How long is it going to take before the Lord returns?' 'How fast are we travelling towards the second coming?' What then evolved in their consciousness has to evolve in ours. We have to learn that the Day of Christ which they were calculating and day-dreaming about has already dawned.

Daily meditation teaches us to live in that Day of Christ, and in the mystery of God it contains, more freely, more fully each day. It isn't that we deny the relative reality of time and space. By living in the present moment, we come to live much more efficiently, reasonably and sensibly in time and space. But we see that they are relative to God who is completely unrestricted by them. Then we begin to see in a Christian vision that the link between this relative reality of the human condition and the pure reality of God is Christ, who is in time but contains time, who is in space but transcends it. Such vision is the outgrowth of experience, of silence. Books and discussions use metaphors to point to it. But there comes a point where we have to be silent, leaving metaphors behind and entering the pure and simple reality. So we say our word. And we become silent. So we learn day by day, year by year, as time passes, that this journey is of a moment. We arrive before we know we have got there, sometimes even before we know we have left. St Paul writes: 'I will unfold a mystery: we shall not all die, but we shall all be changed in a flash, in a twinkling of an eye.'

We resist the journey. We resist the power that draws us along the way, because we know that the journey leads to the death of part of us. Yet if we can be only a little open, a little faithful, then the power that draws us on is sensed to be stronger than our resistance. At any point it is always a little stronger than our resistance. So, despite ourselves, we do make the journey, and as we grow we come to understand more clearly what St Paul means. We perceive that death is an awakening and that we are changed in the brief moment before we cease to be, in the twinkling of an eye. Father John said that the Kingdom is not a place but an experience. To regard it as a place is to have our consciousness limited by metaphor. To approach it as an experience is to be free for the full knowledge of the Kingdom. The experience is of seeing everything in that twinkling of an eye, in the moment of Christ, in the Day of Christ, the day of the perpetual meridian.

So, if we use the metaphor of a journey to try to understand why we meditate, we should complement and correct it with the metaphor of vision. Meditation leads us to purity of heart, and Jesus tells us that this is happiness, blessedness, because in that purity of heart we see God. 'Seeing God' is a metaphor. The vision of God cannot be the vision of an object. We cannot know God as an object. It is not the vision that we have, for example, when we look at a beautiful view, nor when we look at a monstrance on the altar. The contemplative vision is not bound by the categories of subject and object any more than the journey is bound by time and space. The key to understanding this lies in the most important human experience: of knowing and being known, the human experience of love. Our vision of another is utterly altered when we realize that they see us. The barriers of egoism, the subject–object barriers, collapse. These are the barriers that Christ is described as removing when he removed the walls that separate all the peoples.

The vision of God is seeing God with the vision with which he sees us, the same vision in which he alone sees himself. Only God can see God, or those in God. We can come to understand a little of what that means by knowing that love is a sharing in the self-knowledge of another. The only precondition for this journey of vision is that we have stopped looking at ourselves and have become still. If meditation leads us to see Christ in everyone and everywhere, it is because it has taught us to look away from ourselves and to live by looking away from ourselves. So we come to understand that we can only see Christ in the Spirit, that the Spirit is both the journey of Jesus to the Father and the vision in which the Father sees the Son.

Knowledge and Experience

We probably begin to meditate because we feel there is a hidden potential within us yet to be realized. We decide to meditate because no other way seems open to bring that deep potency to full actuality. Meditation can spring that buried power because it is the way of knowledge. So many of the other ways open to us are merely ways of experience and we are always looking for experiences. On the way of meditation we are not looking for experiences, because the way of knowledge is the better part.

Following the way gradually informs us of the existence of two kinds of self-knowledge corresponding to two ways of approaching experience.

Before we begin to meditate our principal form of self-knowledge informs us about our limitations. It tells us about all the ways we fail. It highlights the ways we fall short of ideals, whether ideals we set ourselves or that others set for us. It is the self-knowledge that suggests what we would like to do or be but somehow can't. Evidently, it is not a pleasant kind of self-knowledge to live with. Not surprisingly, we want to distract ourselves from it. By spending too much time in that kind of self-knowledge life begins to lose its flavour, and the journey becomes one into cynicism or even despair. Such self-knowledge is born of self-analysis, judging, or examining ourselves, usually by other people's standards, seeking others' approval. It is that most common form of self-knowledge today: the knowledge of personal inadequacy. A monstrous self-consciousness is formed in us until we eventually feel that in self-knowledge of this kind we can never get to know our true

selves. So then a duality is set up within between the inner
reality of the unknown self, the hidden potential, and the outer
reality of the ego, which is our partially, inadequately realized
potential. Such a dualistic vision of life drains life of meaning
because it robs life of unity. Our life is wounded and fractured
because we are divided within ourselves.

Then by grace we are led to meditate. We all begin in
different ways. Somehow the seed is dropped into our hearts,
at some point it begins to germinate and eventually we begin
to meditate seriously. Then the other kind of self-knowledge
begins to dawn. It is an awareness, no longer of limitation, but
of burgeoning potential. It is not just fantasy, dreaming what
we might be like, but rather knowing it to be potential that we
personally possess as a presence within us, as gift. We realize
the potential of selfhood by accepting the gift of being.

This is why Father John described meditation as the way to
accept the gift of our own being. As we follow the way of
accepting the gift, life acquires the dynamic of an expanding
mystery. From being a mere problem it expands into mystery.
A problem is a knot in life. The untying of the knot is the
revealing of mystery. An essential characteristic of a mystery
is that it cannot be analysed. Our own being is a mystery. We
can enter into the mystery but we can't analyse it. We can't
dissect it. In analysing it we miss its meaning. The livingness
of it slips through our fingers and it gets tangled up into being
merely another problem.

Most people in our society conduct a frantic search for
mystery, often seeking it outside themselves. The first step of
wisdom is to know that the first level of mystery we can
encounter is our own being. That is the door into *the* mystery.
Entering into the mystery of our own being is also gaining the
new kind of self-knowledge, no longer based on self-analysis or
self-observation but on humility, reverence and self-acceptance.

Why should meditation be this way? Because the strange
thing is that we can only accept ourselves by letting go of
ourselves. Meditation is simply entering into the mystery of our
own being by letting go of ourselves. How, in real life and in

actual practice, do we come to this higher kind of self-knowledge? We arrived at the other kind, the self-analytical kind, by thinking about ourselves, by examining ourselves. But this kind of self-knowledge, the real kind, we arrive at by a reverse process. We arrive at it by turning the attention off ourselves, by forgetting ourselves.

We can forget many things. It is amazing in the course of a day how many things we can forget. It is amazing how we can forget the most important things, the most pressing, urgent things that need to be done. Sometimes we even forget our own name and who we are. Yet one thing we find it almost impossible to forget is *ourselves*, which is the one thing we most need to forget. To forget ourselves means to let go of our self-consciousness, to be simple, to *be*. We know (this is the innate perception of the hidden potential we have) that we have to let go of self-consciousness if we are to be free to experience life as an expanding mystery rather than as a problem. There is no growth in consciousness, or growth in the Spirit until we have begun to cut loose from self-consciousness. The vital question is, 'How do we do it?' The simple answer is, 'say your mantra'. To meditate you don't have to be very clever or wise or perceptive, only serious enough to begin and then humble enough to continue. It is the saying of the word that leads into that unity of consciousness we call simplicity. When we say the mantra, we leave the problem of life behind and enter its mystery. We leave self-consciousness behind and enter real self-knowledge simply by saying the mantra faithfully every day, each morning and each evening, and being faithful to the consequences it creates.

What does it take? It takes very simple qualities. First of all, it takes humility to allow yourself to do something as simple as that. It takes a certain amount of trust, because you have to do it for yourself for some time before you can verify the claims made for it. It takes a certain amount of courage to turn the attention off ourselves, even for a short space of time. And it takes perseverance, the spiritual and psychological stamina to continue. The wonder is that everything we need to make the

journey is given to us because the power by which we make it
is not our own but Christ's. We don't propel ourselves out of
our self-consciousness. It is the energy of Christ, his love, that
takes us beyond ourselves.

That is the humility of meditation. Perhaps that is the most
important quality we need, an intelligent humility. It is humility
that allows us to follow a way where we know we are opening
mind and heart to a mystery greater than ourselves, to a power
of love stronger than our egoism. It is only necessary to begin
in humble simplicity, and then the power we need to continue is
available to us. Simplicity is all contained in saying the mantra.

Simplicity is the knowledge St Paul speaks of in his Letter
to the Ephesians. He is praying that out of the treasures of his
glory the Father may

> . . . grant you strength and power through his Spirit in your
> inner being, that through faith Christ may dwell in your
> hearts in love. With deep roots and firm foundations may
> you be strong to grasp with all God's people, what is the
> breadth and length and height and depth of the love of Christ
> and to know it though it is beyond knowledge. So may you
> attain to fullness of being, the fullness of God himself. (Eph.
> 3:16–19)

The Light of the Self

One of the great causes of sadness and suffering is the inability to communicate. So often what we try to express or the medium of expression distorts what we feel or mean. The repeated failure to communicate can accumulate a terrible sense that we can never communicate what we really feel or mean. If we feel that our real self is permanently isolated from others and our deepest feelings are prevented from communication beyond ourselves then we are in the isolation which underlies all loneliness and fear. One of the most powerful effects of meditation is that it confronts this bitter sense of isolation directly. That is why fairly soon after you begin to meditate you begin to get 'cold feet' and to feel, 'This is too much'. To confront that sense of isolation directly is uncomfortable. It may well have caused much suffering and so it has probably been suppressed, rationalized, come to terms with. We have settled for isolation.

By meditating we raise it up again and this time there is nowhere to hide. There is no way to distract ourselves from it if we are meditating. Meditation exposes as a hard and essential truth that if you want to be fully human you must face the fact that if we cannot communicate our real self to others it is because we haven't yet made contact with it ourselves. If we feel isolated from those around us it is because we are isolated from ourselves. Only when we know who we are and so can be who we are, can we communicate ourselves to others. As you meditate you come into contact with your real communicable self. Doing that requires a certain amount of real work in perseverance in meditation.

Perseverance will make us ask the question, 'What does in

fact block us from our real self?' Meditation gives us a very
simple answer. Not an easy answer, but a simple one. 'Nothing.'
Nothing lies between us and our real selves. Nothing anyway
except the false idea that something does lie between them.
The false idea is what we call the ego. And the ego, which is
the cause of all the sadness of isolation, exists only as an
illusion, as nothing at all. It is simply a distorted perception of
reality, the false lens which blurs our vision and makes us
misinterpret ourselves and others in double vision. Nothing lies
between our real self and ourself because obviously *we* are our
real self. To realize that is realization. To experience our inner
light as one with the reality of the Divine Light is called enlightenment. To realize it we have to learn how to be ourself and
to leave behind the false idea, to correct the blurred vision of
the ego. The ego is a mistake.

The problem is to locate the cause of the mistake so that we
can correct it and leave it behind, locate the root and pull it
out. But to try to search for it would be only to strengthen it.
We should seek the truth not the mistake. So we meditate, and
when we meditate we leave behind this false idea, because we
leave *all* ideas behind. Meditation as a way is as simple as our
real self.

There is discipline involved in learning to meditate. There
are some very simple practices to learn. And like any other
kind of art, they take a certain amount of practice and perseverance. We have to sit still, to sit upright, with the back straight,
to close the eyes lightly, to sit relaxed but alert and then silently,
interiorly to say our mantra.

At each time of meditation morning and evening we shuffle
off another layer of self-consciousness. First we learn to leave
all ideas behind. Then at the next layer of consciousness we
detach from the imagination and we leave all images behind.
When we have done that, we are simply ourselves, unlayered
and naked. This is what Jesus called 'poverty of spirit'. And
he said that the 'poor in spirit' are happy. All sadness is left
behind, and we are spiritually happy because 'ours is the

Kingdom of God' where the real self shines forth in its own light.

It is a beautiful poverty of spirit. It is an invigorating path to follow. If there are times when it is rough that doesn't stop it being happy, beautiful and peaceful. It is a grand poverty because it sets us free to see the light of our real self and to know that we are that light. The mantra takes us through the layers of thought, language and imagination to the pure light of full consciousness. The mantra is very simple. It is like the bleep that leads a plane to land through fog, for by following the bleep the plane stays on course. If you have worked with computers you might think of it as like the little pointer on the screen which is called the cursor and which both follows and leads the mind of the programmer. Where this little dot is, there too is the operator. The mantra is simply the focal point that leads us to the centre where the light of the real self shines out. As you continue to meditate you may not feel this happening during the times of meditation but don't worry and don't look for anything to happen, any light to shine or words to sound or anything at all to happen. If you persevere then your life itself will slowly but deeply shine with that inner light you are uncovering and you will know that the light is there in everything.

Father John said that all we have to lose on the way of meditation are our limitations. The greatest brake on our expansion of spirit is the illusion that we are divided from our real self. As we lose that limitation we gain knowledge of the truth that we are one with ourself, with each other and with God. We learn what St John in his Gospel and Letters showed he had learnt, that the light which shines in us is the Light of Christ, the realized Light which enlightens everyone who comes into the world. 'Here is the message we heard from him and pass on to you: that God is light and in him there is no darkness . . . if we walk in the light as he himself is in the light then we share together a common life' (1 John 1:5–7).

The way into that light shining at the centre of our self is a way of poverty but of beautiful poverty. It is a way of simplicity summed up not only in theory but in practice by the saying of the mantra. That is all we have to do, commit ourselves to the poverty of the mantra. And to live out the consequences of that commitment in our daily life.

Happiness

I think one of the reasons for Father John's influence and authority was that he could convince people they could be happy. He made it seem a reasonable hope that you could be free and joyful, that you could grow and that life had meaning. It is a rare gift to be able to convince anyone of something so positive. It is much easier to convince a room full of people that life is about suffering than that it is about joy. No one needs to be convinced that life has an unhappy ending or that it involves grief. But we all find it very difficult to be persuaded that real life is about living in a spirit of joy. That doesn't mean to say that he ever underestimated what was demanded of us if we are going to know that joy. He certainly saw, for example, that one of the great problems of our society is that we don't see life as tragic and, therefore, can't see it as joyful. We see life in terms of pleasure, or distraction, not in terms of commitment. Therefore, we don't experience joy; therefore, we can't believe that joy is what life is about.

In *Word into Silence*, when he is introducing meditation, he says, 'As this idea may be a novel one and indeed even sound rather strange, let me repeat the basic technique of meditation . . .' And that was his approach, to repeat what sounded strange to us, to repeat what sounded novel. Novelty can have something very attractive about it. But the novelty in itself is always deceptive because nothing can retain its novelty for long. If we try to live out of the shallow experience of novelty then we inevitably live a life of distraction. We are always looking to see how we can ride the crest of novelty and so are looking always at ourselves and our reactions. And we're running – running from the fear of what will happen if we let the novelty fade and look directly into the heart of the experience. Repetition makes novelty fade and draws us into a deep familiarity with the experience itself. Familiarity is that sense of belonging that St Benedict calls stability, and it is the only secure context for happiness, for joy, because it develops rootedness in reality. To go for novelty is to be constantly uprooting ourselves, emotionally, psychologically, spiritually. This is as true with regard to human relationships, as it is for any spiritual discipline.

The result of repetition is rootedness and as the roots sink down deeper, the life force of joy begins to flow through them. It is joy that begins to give life a spirit of happiness which is not just the result of entertainment or superficial stimulation but of a power coming up from beneath. The rising energy of love, of well-being, of confidence in the meaning of our experience transforms the surface. We learn from meditation that the surface circumstances of our life can never be changed from the surface. They can only be changed from beneath, from the roots upwards. So, as one of the first hurdles of faith, we have to face the fact that we don't believe we can be happy because the experience of happiness has been restricted to the consequences of surface changes. We all know that those changes don't last for very long and any efforts to change those circumstances can so readily become self-distraction. Soon life becomes debilitatingly sad because we are no longer even trying for happiness but to distract ourselves from unhappiness. Then there appears the other hurdle of faith which has to be cleared many times along the course, that we don't think we *should* be happy. Everyone has been exposed to a negative view of self which insinuates that we are unworthy to be happy or that it is unfair to be happy while there is inequality or injustice in the world. Then in order to cope with those problems of faith, we have to understand that it isn't happiness we are searching for but truth. If we search for happiness then we are merely serving ourselves. But if we search for truth with all the strength, commitment and passion we are capable of, then we will serve the truth. And by finding ourselves in the truth we will learn to love ourselves by learning that the truth loves us. Truth is a person, and so truth creates love.

The monastic life has as its primary aim to give the self wholeheartedly to the search for the truth. This is the search for God, and the self discovers it in itself as well as in the life of the community as the personal encounter with Jesus. The wonder of the new monasticism is that it is characterized, not by distraction or busyness, but by a deep-rooted joyfulness. That is why Fr. John would ask people who came, 'Are you ready for the joy that can be yours?' It is a challenging question because we are ready for sadness. We are ready for compromise and for second-best. But it is very demanding to be told to get ready for the absolute, for full joy, fullness of life, the best not the second-best. Fear of joy is one of the main reasons why we falter on the way and why our faith needs to be continually strengthened by each other in the Lord. We are frightened of the intensity of joy. It takes us into a new realm of experience where the centre of consciousness is no longer me and my search for happiness but the other and the enjoyment of happiness. The prospect of joy frightens us because we have got used to being busy in superficially searching for happiness and have forgotten how to enjoy it. We must learn the art of prayer in order to master the art of living: how to accept joy and how, in times of trial or tragedy, to wait for the joy to return at a deeper and more rooted level of being. Meditation continuously reminds us that the joy of the Lord is in *depth* of being. It is waiting for us to release it and we release it by learning the courage to seek it in the depths.

Reverence

Religious people tend to be more self-conscious than others. And if we are honest about our self-consciousness we should see its connection with a certain lack of reverence in our religious life. We may indeed be surprised that at the most sacred moments in our religious life our spirit of reverence is shamefully hollow. A busy, noisy irreverence in our churches is certainly something that non-Christians often remark upon. They remark for example on the lack of silence or of physical stillness. They often remark too about the amount of time spent in asking God for things we want.

This does not mean that we should never move in our seats, or that words are not an enriching part of religious worship. But I think meditation changes our attitude to worship because it teaches from within our own experience that the God we worship is present and that it is his presence that we are worshipping. Meditation makes our religious life more reverential because it teaches us, through experience of his indwelling Presence, that it is *in* his Presence that we worship his Presence. We are no less in him than he is in us. In the interpenetration of his consciousness with ours we know because we are known. The most natural response to any experience in which we know and are known is reverential silence. Silence leads deeper into mutual knowledge.

When we understand worship in the light of mutual, interpenetrating Presence we see that any words we may use are not for God's benefit but for our own, to prepare us to enter the silence of his Presence more deeply and reverently. The idea that words and prayers of petition are addressed to ourselves and are not for informing God is found in St Augustine. Such words work when they lead to a silence which reveals the presence in an ever fuller consciousness. It is through that revelation that we learn real reverence. Many of us were taught reverence as children through fear. We were forced to 'behave properly' and to conform. What was not taught us in that approach was the essential fact that a spirit of reverence is natural to us, an integral function of consciousness and an indispensable quality of true humanity, because lacking it we fall into mere superficiality and superstition.

True reverence is learned by becoming aware of a consciousness greater than our own. Think of those moments when you have become aware of a higher other consciousness and you can easily imagine that the response to it might be not reverence but fear. It is part of the human condition that an element of fear is indeed present because what is greater than us can destroy us. In the Christian revelation however the fear of annihilation is transcended, because we know that to open our heart to this greater consciousness is to know simultaneously that it knows us and its knowledge is love. Our self-knowledge is humbling because God's presence teaches us that he loves and knows us more deeply than a human consciousness can love or know itself. The opening of consciousness to God is both knowledge of God and of ourselves. We can do it because we have been empowered to do it through the consciousness of Jesus. His consciousness is so irreversibly open to the Father that it is one with him, and when in silence we know his human consciousness dwelling in ours we are awakened by his love, his knowledge of the Father and of us.

That is why we come to know ourselves and each other by this way of meditation so much more deeply and reverently than by any way of analysis or introspection. Self-knowledge acquired through analysis or introspection is only knowledge of self – I knowing me – and is limited to the dimension of a single reflection in a mirror. But the knowledge of self awakened in meditation is God's knowledge of the self and so is also knowledge of an other to the self. The dimension of self-knowledge in God involves relationship and so is infinite. We experience ourselves wondrously and humbly as mysteries dwelling in his mystery, knowing with his knowledge everything he discloses to us through love's consciousness. Thus any true knowledge we have of ourselves is gift. It is God's knowledge of us which can never be the result of curious inquiry. It is never objectified or analytical knowledge and so proves the impossibility of a private wisdom. His knowledge is love, unifying because self-giving. So, to know ourselves is both to love and sacrifice ourselves because his knowledge of us is his sacrificial love of us.

A sense of reverence is born in a gasp of wonder. Plato said that the love of wisdom begins with wonder. Wonder is also the condition of prayer, which is a state of consciousness open to something greater than ourselves, not in fear, but in reverence and love. Wonder as the condition of prayer is not being baffled by not understanding; it is a state of certain knowledge and of clear vision. It is knowing by seeing intensely and wholly but it also involves knowing that what we see is part of the whole mystery. The humility of the wonder of prayer is knowing that we have to open our consciousness further and that we can never know fully until we have transcended the last limits of our own consciousness to become one with the greater consciousness that can be known only by its own self-knowledge.

Knowing what we see to be only a small part of the whole is still an exhilarating and enlivening experience. We know implicitly that we are expanding and that we will one day see the whole. We will know even as we are known. This is why, as strange as it may sound, you can tell where there is real reverence by the presence of a spirit of joy. Reverence and wonder are expressed in the stillness and silence of meditation but from that stillness and silence comes the spirit of pure life, the bliss of God, the delight of spiritual knowledge. Liberty of spirit and a deeply rooted joy form the experience of wonder and our natural response of reverence fills us with a deep confidence. This is the confidence with which a person preaches the Gospel and which St Paul urged his early communities to work for, to nourish and give thanks for. It is not merely human self-confidence, not the complacency given by insurance policies but a christocentric confidence whose source lies beyond ourselves.

Confidence, enjoyment and detachment are all closely bound together in spiritual knowledge and are generated by the experience of wonder. We use so many words. We hear the same words, the same ideas, so many times a day that they become blunted for us. But many people will remember how they could hear the words of St Paul read by Father John as if they were hearing them for the first time. That was wonder. Without wonder we forget that the reality we are talking of and worshipping *is* real, *is* present. Reverence and wonder can grow only out of a direct contact with real Presence. Otherwise, we remain locked at the level of indirect contact, talking *about*, thinking *about*. We then inevitably become self-consciously concerned with the way we talk, the way we express it, the way we come across; and so develops religious self-importance. The next step is to become argumentative or condemnatory. This is the great curse and tendency of religious people, the consequence of losing reverence.

Yet the way from self-importance to reverence is so simple. We don't have to try to engineer direct contact with God because it has already been made. That is the incarnation, the Word made flesh. We don't have to try to argue our way into that greater Consciousness because it has already taken up its dwelling within us, not by argument but by love. Meditation is simply knowing that.

This is how St Paul talks on Christian knowledge in the First Letter to the Corinthians,

Is there knowledge? It will vanish away; for our knowledge and our prophecy alike are partial, and the partial vanishes when wholeness comes. When I was a child, my speech, my outlook, and my thoughts were all childish. When I grew up, I had finished with childish things. Now we see only puzzling reflections in a mirror, but then we shall see face to face. My knowledge now is partial; then it will be whole, like God's knowledge of me. In a word, there are three things that last forever: faith, hope and love; but the greatest of them all is love. (1 Cor. 13:8–13)

Power and Love

Reading a collection of letters from Rudyard Kipling to his children recently I was struck by a definition of his love for his children who, by comparison with him anyway, were remarkably ungifted and unexceptional. With them he was able to 'expend an inexhaustible passion on apparently worthless objects'. It reminded me of a remark about the monastic life as being where one bestows an unaccountable zeal on things of no account. Similar to that is the inexhaustible passion with which we follow the journey of meditation, the unaccountable zeal we give to the little task of saying the mantra. In this love for one's children, one's community, for God, we encounter a love that is pure because it is selfless, and selfless because it has renounced power.

One of the dominant values of our society is power. It is taken for granted that power is automatically a good value because it suggests the capacity to control or direct events or people and it is felt to be obviously better to have this capacity than not to have it. It is recognized, of course, that it can be used for good or for evil, but we are nevertheless asked to believe by contemporary conditioning that power over others is good. It seems good to see ourselves in control and we assume that the best good is when we are in absolute control. Not surprisingly, meditation challenges that assumption as it challenges the entire scale of our values. It directs the light of Christ and of the gospel teaching upon ordinary lives, and it transforms the scale of accepted values by exposing them to the light.

It directs light on the *actual* scale of values by which we lead our lives and reveals that there are in practice usually two scales of values, an ideal and an actual. We believe, for example, that we should love our enemies. It is an ideal we accept. But the actual scale of values by which we live allows us to qualify that. We are allowed to show them that they are our enemies. We can let them know what they are really like and make them pay the price for being our enemies. Our actual scale of values is almost totally self-centred, while the ideal scale is, of course, selfless and other-centred.

Meditation makes it difficult to justify living on two scales for long. It reconciles them, although not without the pain of self-knowledge. On the self-centred scale we are constantly compromising and giving ourselves the benefit of the slightest doubt, indulging ourselves. But that leads ultimately to a sustained moral failure that results not even in pleasure but in self-rejection. It is that loss of authenticity from which we are redeemed by Christ when we are open to his power. Meditation can redeem us from that bankruptcy of moral failure and inauthenticity, because prayer is an essential part of the whole Christian work of redemption. It is an essential channel of the spirit of Christ. On the self-centred scale we believe that we have power over ourselves. We believe that we have the final word on what we should be, what we should do, how we should do it. We have the choice. It is our basic right.

But in meditation, provided we follow the path all the way, we find that we are renouncing that arrogance. We are renouncing self-centredness and so we are renouncing power over ourselves – not because we have given notional assent to an ideal scale of values, but because this is what we are actually doing by saying the mantra. That is why it is so important to continue saying it. There is a great temptation to regain power for ourselves, and the easiest way is to stop saying the mantra. It helps us if we remember that what we are renouncing in saying the mantra is an illusion because we don't really have ultimate power over ourselves. The ego as the spinner of all illusion insists (and sometimes with great persuasiveness, learning and intelligence) that we do have ultimate power. It says that I am the one in control of my direction and growth. But if we listen to the ego's voice we lose all direction and cease to grow.

The power to control, which we think is such a natural good, is shown to be not so good by the fact that it can so easily turn into violence. If we think we have ultimate power over ourselves we are only one step from saying that we deserve the same power over others, 'for their own good'. Meditation is a renunciation of all power, a complete poverty of spirit and in that poverty we encounter instead the only power there is, the power of love. In our deepest selves, at the most significant moments of our life, we know that is the only real power. We forget it perhaps because such pure love is rare in our experience, but its rarity does not reduce its truthfulness.

Meditation gradually transforms both values and action because it teaches that the only real power is God's and he is love. We learn that power is good in human relationships, in social relationships, only when it is his power exercised directly by itself, love in itself, the energy of God investing the human condition. And wherever God's love enters the human condition there is Christ. If we try to claim this power as our own, or if we even try to possess love, we make it de-creative. Thus love can degenerate into violence; it may wound rather than heal. Because it is so easy to do that, the only way to make sure that we are not usurping that power is to renounce it, to renounce all power, as Jesus renounced all power in the absolute poverty of the cross – power over his friends as well as over his enemies. In doing this he manifested the power of God as the Father's love, and he revealed it as not rare at all but present everywhere at all times, the ground of being. The result of his renunciation was not, as we so often fear it will be for ourselves, failure or destruction but the ultimate manifestation of God's power in man which is the resurrection, man fully empowered by God.

The mantra, the little thing upon which we bestow that unaccountable zeal and inexhaustible passion, teaches all this upon the real scale of values in life. Its way of teaching is to take us into the experience of Jesus: renunciation, poverty and the resurrection. The signs of that experience can be recognized on the real scale of values present in all relationships as the spirit of love. This is a power over which we have no control because it is God, but it invests and expands every relationship beyond desire, beyond possessiveness and beyond the ego's attempt to control. In every relationship, personal or social, we begin to recognize the presence of that power which takes us not just into sympathy with others but into union with them. This is the nature of love. By its renunciation of power over the other it becomes *one* with the other. God himself did not merely sympathize with the human condition but identified himself with it and became man in Jesus.

That understanding of the power of God is the great proclamation of the Gospel and this is how St Paul expresses it in the Letter to the Philippians:

> God knows how I long for you all, with the deep yearning of Christ Jesus himself. And this is my prayer, that your love may grow ever richer and richer in knowledge and insight of every kind, and may thus bring you the gift of true discrimination. Then on the Day of Christ you will be flawless and without blame, reaping the full harvest of righteousness that comes through Jesus Christ, to the glory and praise of God. (Phil. 1:8–11)

Learning to Receive

Much is revealed about the tradition of meditation in general by looking at the particular teaching about the mantra. John Main expresses it like this when he introduces the mantra in *Word into Silence*: 'Choosing your word or mantra is of some importance . . . You should choose your mantra in consultation with your teacher. If you have no teacher to help you, then you should choose a word that has been hallowed over the centuries by our Christian tradition.' What is clear here is that whether you start with a teacher or on your own, you start because something has been *given* to you. The mantra itself is given to us, either personally or by the tradition, and so the starting point for the journey is a gift. Progress on the journey is fidelity to that gift which means learning how to receive it and to recognize the beauty, the wonder, the infinite generosity contained in the gift. In our materialistic experience gifts have a limited time span. After a while they seem to lose the power of novelty they had at the moment we received them. In the spiritual realm the gift increases in power because we are able to see more and more clearly the generosity behind it. Such a gift is never lost. Incredibly, that tiny little gift of the mantra becomes for us, as it were, the channel of the infinite generosity of God. Our progress is in fidelity to the gift. We have to learn how to receive a gift just as we have to learn how to be loved.

Most religious and other problems arise because we want to be the first to love. We want to be the giver of a gift. Real wisdom as well as real humility (which is the only wisdom) shows us that first it is necessary to learn to be loved before we can love and to receive before we can give. Learning to receive the gift requires everything that we've got to give. There is no half-way in receiving a gift. Everything we have got has to be open to the gift.

On the way there are many ordeals, challenges and tests of faith, both externally and interiorly. We can doubt the adequacy of the gift. We can say, 'Am I missing out on something? If I give everything I've got in accepting this gift, maybe I am missing out on other gifts that might be available to me.' And then there's complexity. We look at ourselves and see all the different facets and levels, all the areas that need to be fulfilled and we say, 'Aren't I selling myself short just by accepting this little gift? Will it be adequate enough to fulfil me?' And then there is plain restlessness when we say to ourselves, 'Couldn't we speed this up? Couldn't we find a way, or a place, or a book or anything to speed up the whole process?' There is no one who doesn't experience those challenges. But at any point we know how to deal with the challenge. We say the mantra. We accept the gift.

Many people, when they are going through those problem times, stop saying the mantra and therefore miss the wonder and generosity of the gift. It is the saddest thing that a person can do. They lose the opportunity at the very moment when it is offered in its greatest generosity, because those times of testing are simply times of deepening. They are times when we have to say the mantra in the purest faith and most childlike trust, with the strongest courage, not for what we get out of it but simply because the gift has been given and it would be ungracious to throw the gift back at that moment.

By remaining faithful to the mantra we remain faithful to the whole pilgrimage which the mantra symbolizes and spiritually contains. It is a pilgrimage to integrity and fullness, an utter joy which nothing interior or exterior can shake. It is the journey to the place where there is nothing at all false in us, but where there is simply love. And the mantra makes it wonderfully simple, because it shows that the pilgrimage is not something projected into the future but something that occurs in the present moment. The pilgrimage is not about 'where am I going

to be at this time next year? Where will I be in ten years time?'
The pilgrimage is 'I am here. I *am here.*' When a person is
rooted in the present moment and needs to turn his thoughts
or concerns to the future he is not fantasizing. He is discovering
that the future is contained in the mystery of the present
moment of God – which is the dimension we enter into through
our own heart. Then he begins to understand the prophetic
vision every Christian is called to by seeing time contained in
the present moment of God and the shape of the future in the
structure of the present. Saying the mantra, learning to remain
faithful to the gift, is learning to hear and see, to know and
love what *is*. There is more joy in that hearing, seeing, knowing
and loving than we have yet the capacity for. Joy expands our
heart and our mind until we lose ourselves in the heart and the
mind of Christ.

We ask ourselves inevitably, 'How is it that I can believe this
and yet somehow fail to act upon it? Why is it that I know it
makes sense, I *do* believe it, it makes more than sense, it gives
me the feeling of truth, and yet there seems to be a falling
short?' It is because hearing and seeing with the mind is inadequate. We have to hear and see also with the heart. Meditation
is the work of opening the eye and the ear of the heart. Work
takes time. It requires stability. It asks for faith. It demands
courage. But when the eye and the ear of the heart are open
then there is an end to duplicity and duality. There is no more
failure and no falling short, because when the heart sees and
hears there is perfect response. A knowledge is born which is
not that of the outsider or the observer but is of one who
participates in what is known. The Knowing One is God who
calls us to know him, to see him and to love him by being
totally one with him.

Depth

One of the dangers of talking a lot about spiritual matters is that one finds oneself the prisoner of a vocabulary. A word that can be used too often is 'depth'. Yet it is a metaphor that can help to make understood and fully personal the journey that we are on. These words from *Moment of Christ* clarify the metaphor:

> . . . it is the faithful repetition of our word that integrates our whole being. It does so because it brings us to the silence, the concentration, the necessary level of consciousness that enable us to open our mind and heart to the work of the love of God in the depth of our being.

It brings us to 'the necessary level of consciousness'. There is the constant danger that we think about these levels of consciousness but fail to open them up. As long as we think or read about them we remain at a cerebral level, the level of thought and imagination. This is an important level but not the level of consciousness needed to open up the centre where the love of God is purely itself, where it begins in us and therefore where we begin, because it is out of that love that we are created. It is at that level that self is lost and found. Incredible as it may sound, it goes beyond our own created beginning into the depth of God. And that is the journey that everyone is invited, challenged to make. The only reason for talking, thinking or reading about depths of consciousness is to make it *real* and to help to clear away some of the false or cluttered ideas that make it difficult to get through that narrow gate –

to chuck out some of the baggage that has accumulated over the years, to simplify, to make ourselves more available.

A metaphor like 'depth of being' can be useful because it suggests that our own experience can become more than merely individual. We need no longer see experience merely as 'my journey, my holiness, my salvation'. We see instead that to make the journey is to leave the word 'my' and 'mine' behind. In recognizing our experience as part of the universal human journey something very important is discovered: that life only has meaning within the *whole*, the whole human family, the whole plan of God, the whole creation created in the Word and returning in the Word. That is the beginning of conversion, of turning around and travelling back to the source. As we travel back we cast off the exclusiveness that prevents us from taking our unique place in the whole. The amazing experience is of losing our life, despite our fear of losing it, despite our resistance to losing it and the fight we put up to keep it and all the tricks we play to hang on to it. We discover that the uniqueness we possess is not because we are excluded or cut off from the whole but because we share in a common origin. Uniqueness is in similitude rather than in difference. The conversion is from being isolated beings into beings fully present to all other beings by sharing in the personal nature of God, the relationship of the Trinity which is the perfect relationship and of which all relationships are expressions. A basic paradox gives liberty to our lives; union differentiates. The deeper the union, the more fully personal we become.

It is precisely this union that is found in the depth of the personal self. Experience of a union that is beyond thought, imagination and language means that it can only be known in silence. As soon as we try to analyse it or verbalize it, we feel that we have passed out of it. At least we are not fully present in it because it demands total attention. There is no place, therefore, at the time of our meditation for *expression*, for talking or conceptualizing. Everything has to be in pure attendance on that great Mystery that is found in the depth. Out of the pure attention of prayer comes the continuous mindfulness

of a Christian consciousness throughout every activity of the
day. However trivial or ephemeral, every minute and action
has meaning and sacredness because in that moment and
through that act the Divine communion reveals itself.

By such knowledge we grow. Every relationship that is alive,
that is loving, has to grow: love is growth into union. The love
of God is eternally expansive. Whether we like it or not, there
is no place to settle down and hang on to what has been gained.
Everything has to be renounced so that more can be received.
This explains the poverty and the simplicity of the mantra as
it does the joy and freedom of the Christian life. But it is
demanding. Having got onto this journey we discover that we
are involved in something greater than self. It draws us on by
an attraction that can only be resisted by egoism and the only
way to resist it is to turn away from it, back to the true self.
Egoism is such an unpleasant prospect that in the long term it
is doomed but in the meanwhile it is easy to remain incomplete
and opt for a partial degree of isolation, to waive the right to
be free. It seems relatively easier to remain with the limitations
we know so well and which account for so much of our self-
rejection. But we are called on to something so demanding that
it must be pure love. Only such love would demand the *whole*
person and summon everything hidden out of hiding. True
selfhood hides behind the ego, behind limitations, fears and
insecurities. The self is called out from behind all false struc-
tures of personality and to stand simple, free, whole, and utterly
itself before God. Just because this is so demanding it elicits a
response in us. It has actually created a response – Christ.
In his response something very dynamic has entered human
consciousness: the dynamism that ends isolation and raises the
dead. Peace is the energy of Christ in his response to depth,
a peace that we find in union because there is no peace in
isolation.

Because it is so demanding, it can almost seem that peace is
more frightening than the violence we do to ourselves in the
egotistical state (or the violence done to others). Peace at depth
turns our world upside down. We have to enter into a very fine

balance of life, the fine frequency of the Spirit, to find the simplicity and subtlety to respond to Christ's dynamism. To enter into that depth, to open up that depth means becoming vulnerable and remaining vulnerable, not only in prayer but in every part of life. Love creates vulnerability, the vulnerability of compassion or unconditional commitment. Maturely, we also have to learn to be resilient because being vulnerable will mean that we are wounded and we mustn't allow being wounded to close us up again. That particular balance between vulnerability and resilience is part of the unique intellectual, psychological, spiritual amalgam that a human being is. Each one starts from a different kind of imbalance but all are called to the same balance and centrality, the same rootedness in Christ who was wounded but who was resilient in the transcendence of forgiveness.

Imagination

One of the most radical ideas the tradition of meditation advances is that the imagination is the great enemy of prayer. We have to understand what this means, if we are to understand and communicate to our contemporaries the full richness of Christianity and of this journey of the Spirit we follow. What does it mean to say that the imagination hinders prayer?

When you have been meditating for a while you begin to see that meditation is different from all other activities. The attitude formed to meditation is different from the attitude to nearly all other things. With some of the other things it is compatible. With others it is incompatible and eventually we must let go of those things with which it is incompatible. In this gradual but definite way it changes our life. Remaining faithful to the journey is the one necessary thing. 'He who perseveres will be saved.' Everything else unfolds naturally by staying faithful. But how is this so different from the other things in life and yet so involved with them?

Most of our other activities are heavily goal-oriented. We have a definite aim and method, and we assess ourselves according to our success or failure in achieving that goal. To a certain degree all the other things in life are measurable in this way because we can assess the degree to which we have attained our ambitions. To a certain degree therefore all the other things are controllable because they are measurable. We can increase or decrease performance. Most other things in life are consciously concerned with self-improvement or self-gratification. None of these basic approaches can be applied to meditation. No doubt we begin with these attitudes in regard to meditation, but perseverance means that these attitudes are gradually purified. We meditate because it is natural, not to achieve a goal or get a higher rating.

A common quality that all other activities share is that they are closely linked to the working of the imagination. For example, a goal in our life cannot be a goal if it is already achieved. By definition, it is something imagined and so something we project into the future. Assessment and self-evaluation both demand an imagined ideal by which to judge ourselves or others. So the one thing that all these activities have in common is imagination. Every area of our life is to some degree controlled by different processes of the imagination, which is indicated by the way we regard success as tied to a highly developed imagination. An imaginative person is a person most likely to succeed.

As the word itself makes obvious, imagination is concerned with images, and images constitute our immediate world. We cannot live as sane, creative people by ignoring the imagination. We need a healthy, non-obsessive imagination to live well and react creatively among these images. We also know, although it may take us time consciously to realize it, that there is something beyond the images that our immediate experience is made up of. Man has always known this. It is part of his inherent knowledge of God as creator and as his destiny. It is our inherent knowledge that the invisible Spirit of God dwells within us. So this dimension beyond images is what we call 'reality': God who is unseeable. We know also that this is not just latent knowledge. It is dynamic and stimulates us to expand. To know it means to have received a call. Unless we answer that call we cannot enter into full reality or full being. The call is to enter the dimension beyond images and unless we do this, we do not become real. Entering that dimension beyond images obviously means leaving imagination behind.

Here is our problem; for the strongest force of our ordinary consciousness is imagination. Imagination is the power that relates us to the images in the world we live in. We cannot live ordinarily without it. Imagination is the power that plays with these images, making and unmaking all sorts of compounds among them, the creative compounds we call ideals, plans, thoughts, art. This power is so strong that when we try to leave it, it seems to pursue us and even to control us. No doubt that has always been the case, otherwise the great writers on prayer would not have always given so much attention to the necessity and the difficulty of going beyond the imagination.

But it is probably especially difficult in our society where the imagination has formed strong social and psychological mutations and where our imagination is so ruthlessly exploited, so insidiously stimulated and expertly manipulated that it has become obsessively hyperactive.

So the imagination could never be the power by which we meditate. The power by which we meditate is faith. Faith is pure openness, vision purified of images. It is openness to the realm beyond images. The power by which we meditate as Christians is the faith of Christ, his openness to God, his vision of God. That power derives directly from the dimension of reality itself because faith is the power by which God allows himself to be known. For reality is God who is love. That is why the power by which we leave the imagination for reality is love itself.

Opening ourselves to this power and leaving the imagination behind can be a tricky business. We so easily slip back into the imagination. Day-dreaming is the easiest form of consciousness we know. So full of mirrors is the imagination that we can even delude ourselves by imagining what it would be like to leave the imagination behind. We could not as ordinary people do it without the mantra. The mantra is the focal point in our consciousness of the power of faith and love. The first step of faith is saying it and that step is the key that opens the door which is fully opened by love: the faith and power of Christ. Because the mantra focuses faith and love, we say it with an ever clearer faith and purer love.

Beyond the realm of the imagination we enter poverty of spirit. It is a real poverty because the imagination is our greatest treasure, or so it has us imagine before we enter reality.

Leaving the imagination behind is an act of true impoverishment, and it cannot be done just by imagining what it would be like to do it. There is only one way to do it and that is to do it. We become the more fully poor as we enter into the divine dimension, the dimension of reality beyond images. It helps to know at the outset that this is an exciting and adventurous journey into poverty, purity of spirit. No other journey in life compares with it, for as we enter into the dimension of reality, of love beyond images, we meet the person who is love. We come to see, to know and to love the only real image there is. Beside this all other images are reflections. As we leave these images behind we come to know the image of reality itself in whom all images are resolved. We come to know, to see and to love Christ who is the image of God. In this pure vision there can be no confusion, no blurring, because there is no imagination. In that vision everything is radiant with the light of reality itself. We learn to see with clarity in the brightness.

This vision inspired St Paul to write this to the Colossians:

May he strengthen you, in his glorious might, with ample power to meet whatever comes with fortitude, patience, and joy; and to give thanks to the Father who has made you fit to share the heritage of God's people in the realm of light. He . . . brought us away into the kingdom of his dear Son, in whom our release is secured and our sins forgiven. He is the image of the invisible God; his is the primacy over all created things. In him everything in heaven and on earth was created, not only things visible but also the invisible orders of thrones, sovereignties, authorities, and powers: the whole universe has been created through him and for him. (Col. 1:11–17)

The realm of life is the realm beyond images that we enter as we meditate.

Tradition

When teaching, John Main had a quiet yet evident authority.
It was due above all to his quiet but deep and ever-deepening
understanding of what he was part of. And as he became more
unified with what he was a part, and what we are each in our
unique way part of, is the tradition. He says this in *Word into
Silence* about the way of meditation: 'Cassian received this
method as something which was an old established tradition in
his own day and it is an enduring universal tradition.' The
transmission of a tradition becomes authoritative when it has
become personal. The tradition can be passed on through
books, and the printed word is an essential resource for the
work of transmission. But what makes the tradition live is a
personal experience of it, a personal identification with it. In
Christian faith, when we talk about the tradition we aren't
talking about theology, or philosophy. We are not thinking
about ideas. We are actually talking about a person – one who
is alive, enduring and universal – the person of Jesus.

His teaching, the Gospel, is one with him. The true teacher
is always one with his teaching and teaches more and more
simply by being himself. So we can talk about the Christian
tradition as something that *has* to be authenticated in the
personal realm because we can only communicate the tradition,
as we can only reveal the person of Jesus who is the Good
News, from within a personal encounter. The tradition needs
to become one with our personal experience. That is the power
of its transmission, and personal verification has been the
criterion of Christian teachers, like St Paul, right from the
beginning. 'I did not come', he said, 'to speak to you in words

of philosophy or human wisdom but in the power of the Spirit.'
The power of the Spirit is love and that is why Father John
continued by saying that the tradition becomes one with
personal experience in the moment of love, which is the
moment of prayer.

Monasteries are always focal points of the tradition, and
monasticism has an important place in the stream of the Christian tradition because a monastery is a place dedicated as its
first priority to the moment of love. A monastery is thus, in a
sense, timeless and needs detachment from the world to live
the love which is beyond space and time. The real flight from
the world is not a rejection or an escape but an advance into
a new dimension of time and space which enables each monk
to dwell in the moment of Christ and to discover that that
moment of love contains time, all time.

In its social role and significance, monasticism is essentially
classless and timeless, symbolized by the customs of the
monastic life which are passed on down the centuries. But it
is also utterly contemporary. When monasticism becomes a
museum of rites and customs, it ceases to be timeless and
becomes old-fashioned and, therefore, out of touch. When it
is truly timeless it is most prophetically contemporary. The
reason is that the dimension of time in the monastic life is
measured against its times of prayer. What can look like a
mechanical and boring routine, from the outside, is known
from the inside as an expansion of consciousness beyond the
normal limitations of time and space. Continuously returning
to those times of prayer creates the grammar of each day, the
structure of a lifetime. In every prayer period time and eternity
intersect. In our ordinary, fallible, mortal consciousness we are
opened to the consciousness of Jesus dwelling within us. The
intersection of our consciousness with his, sparks the moment
of love, and it becomes increasingly evident that this occurs
not just at the times of prayer but is incarnate in us at all times.
So in a community dedicated to this moment there gradually
grows the awareness of the continuous Presence, unceasing
prayer.

Acquiring any historical or cultural tradition demands work. If you are going to acquire the tradition of English literature or of Sanskrit scriptures it is not enough to have the books on your shelves; you have to work at them. The work of entering the living tradition of the Christian path, which is the life of Jesus, is the work of prayer, and such work is not a time of study but of spiritual awakening. Awakening not through exertion but through stillness is the subtle difference between meditation and other works and activities. Any effort involved is not for the awakening but for the stillness which precedes the awakening. It is creative work and, therefore, demands an integrated life. Discipline and perseverance are demanded. Like all creative work it absorbs our energy but also, once done, it renews our energy. Artists and writers will often go to great lengths to avoid creative work and will do every other kind of activity – business, administration, manual work – to avoid writing or painting. Religious people often avoid their creative work of prayer by saying many prayers, by becoming religiously busy or administrative about their prayer. They can say many prayers just to avoid the creative work of the mantra.

The Christian life also contains the creative work of loving. The moment of love expands out of the times of meditation into ordinary life, ordinary relationships and concerns. And so the creative work of meditation does in a real way continue at all times as the work of love. Love flows from the work of turning away, from self and self-reflection. We can't meditate selflessly and then spend the rest of the time looking at ourselves to see what progress we have made because we continue the direction of other-centredness at all times. In community that means turning. It would be very easy and has often happened in the Christian tradition that to avoid the work of love people take on all other sorts of work – ascetical extremes, fasting, trying to maintain a self-fixated spirit which is seen as constant mindfulness, pseudo-spiritual effort, to avoid the work of turning towards the other. But the work of the mantra makes us humanly honest in the work of love and prevents us avoiding it by distraction, even if that distraction is about becoming holy. We cannot pray at depth and avoid love. In love we meet the other and in meeting the other, we deepen our encounter with Jesus.

Writings of John Main

Word into Silence (London, Darton, Longman and Todd, 1980; New York, Paulist Press, 1981)
Letters from the Heart (New York, Crossroads, 1982)
Moment of Christ (London, Darton, Longman and Todd, 1984; New York, Crossroads, 1984)
The Present Christ (London, Darton, Longman and Todd, 1985; New York, Crossroads, 1985)

Published by the Benedictine Priory of Montreal (also available from the Christian Meditation Centre, London):

Christian Meditation: The Gethsemani Talks (1977)
Christian Mysteries: Prayer and Sacrament (1979)
Death: The Inner Journey (1983)
The Hunger for Prayer (1983)
The Monastic Adventure (1983)
Monastic Prayer and Modern Man (1983)
The Other-Centeredness of Mary (1983)
Community of Love (1984)

Monastic Studies (1984) no. 15, devoted to the life and work of John Main, and the *Communitas* tapes by John Main are available from the Christian Meditation Centre, London, and the Benedictine Priory, Montreal (for addresses see p. xii).